ANALYZING INVESTMENT PROPERTIES

ANDREW W. TOMPOS

Prentice Hall
Upper Saddle River, NJ 07458

Acquisitions Editor: Elizabeth Sugg

Director of Production and Manufacturing: Bruce Johnson

Managing Editor: Mary Carnis

Marketing Manager: Danny Hoyt

Editorial/Production Supervision and Interior Design:
    Inkwell Publishing Services

Cover Design: Miguel Ortiz

Manufacturing Buyer: Marc Bove

© 1999 by Prentice-Hall, Inc.
Simon & Schuster / A Viacom Company
Upper Saddle River, New Jersey 07458

Printed in the United States of America

10 9 8 7 6 5 4 3 2 1

ISBN 0-13-748948-X

Prentice-Hall International (UK) Limited, *London*
Prentice-Hall of Australia Pty. Limited, *Sydney*
Prentice-Hall Canada Inc., *Toronto*
Prentice-Hall Hispanoamericana, S.A., *Mexico*
Prentice-Hall of India Private Limited, *New Delhi*
Prentice-Hall of Japan, Inc., *Tokyo*
Prentice-Hall of Southeast Asia Pte. Ltd., *Singapore*
Editora Prentice-Hall do Brasil, Ltda., *Rio de Janeiro*

DEDICATION

I dedicate this book to my wife, Betty, and my children, Sarah and Jessica, each of whom has caused me to find ways to support their shopping habits. They have certainly been my inspiration to be successful in everything I try. I also would like to thank my mother (Betty), brothers (Dave and J.P.), and sister (Hon) for always supporting me. And to the memory of my Dad, which is always with me.

My newest source of inspiration is my grandson, Willie.

CONTENTS

Some Introduction and Explanation

The material in this book is intended to be used by realtors, buyers, sellers, and anyone having the desire to learn more about purchasing and owning investment properties. A group of problems at the end of each chapter helps you to assess your understanding of the material. The procedures are applicable to any property owned or considered for purchase. The material can actually be applied to an individual's personal situation.

The *realtor* can use the material to list and sell investment properties and feel comfortable in presenting the information on properties in an organized and consistent manner. The procedures are a vital tool for properly representing a listing, both for realtors and buyers.

The *buyer* can use the material to make the critical decision on buying a property. The text assists buyers in arriving at a fair "offer" and/or to adjust the terms of the purchase to achieve a desired return.

The *seller* can make a decision to sell or to keep a property. The analysis of cash flows and returns might indicate that it makes more sense to keep the property and refinance or to borrow against the equity. A very wealthy investor once said, "You can only sell a property once, but rental income is perpetual."

How the material is collected and organized clearly depicts what the property is returning, for review by both accountants and bankers. *Accountants* should be giving advice on tax consequences on cash flow of owning a property. *Bankers* must decide whether to assist an investment by lending the majority of the money for purchase, and they are not going to invest in a property showing bad returns.

This is also an excellent first book for prospective *investors,* who have sat on the sidelines and watched others play the game. By following and understanding the procedures, an investor can make a purchase in no time, bringing another player into the exciting world of real estate ownership.

There are no promises of getting rich quick! There are no slick nothing-down purchases! There are no secret methods to finding and buying good properties! You get an analytical approach for making a decision to buy, sell, or keep an income-producing property. The key is that you will be able to understand and make your own decision!

No assumptions are made as to mathematical background, experience with a calculator, or the number of educational degrees acquired. Having a financial calculator is a must to save time and to better understand concepts. The following list presents definitions and explanations regarding the use of the HP-12C (probably the financial calculator most used in real estate), as well as the keys most commonly used throughout the book:

PV (*present value*): Normally the principal invested, this key could be the amount borrowed as in a mortgage. It is traditionally defined as the value of money today.

FV (*future value*): This is the amount available after earning interest, traditionally the value of money in the future.

i (*interest rate*): The interest rate must be entered on a per-period basis. Traditionally, interest rate is always given on an *annual basis*. Thus, if there are 12 payments in a year and there is a 10% per-year interest rate, the rate per period is found by .10/12 = .83333... per period.

n (*total number of payments*): If there are 12 periods per year and the loan is for 30 years, then $n = 12 \times 30 = 360$.

PMT (*payment*): Normally the mortgage payment, but could be an amount invested on a regular basis.

g (*blue key*): Press to use the blue functions located at the bottom of most keys.

f (*yellow key*): Press to use the yellow functions located above some keys. Also use this key to set the number of decimal places desired on the screen.

STO (*storage key*): Use this key to store information in registers.

RCL (*recall key*): Use RCL to recall information from the registers.

Other keys and functions will be discussed as they are introduced in the chapters. You should understand several procedures before using the calculator. The HP-12C functions primarily like a computer; therefore, it has no equals sign. This tends to bother most users at first, but they easily overcome this feeling with an example. To multiply 5 times 6, proceed as follows:

1. Enter the 5. ("Enter" means to hit the 5 key so that the 5 appears on the screen.)
2. Hit the ENTER key. (This notifies the computer that you are about to perform an operation or function on the 5.)
3. Enter the 6.
4. Hit the times key ($\times$) and the answer will appear.

Calculator Steps to Set Decimal Places

1. Hit the yellow key.
2. Hit the number key that represents how many decimal places you prefer. (For most of the work in this book, use two decimal places, which represent the nearest cent.) Even though the calculator shows only two places on the screen, it keeps in its memory the exact number for as many places as it can hold.

**Calculator Steps to
Clear the Calculator**

1. Hit yellow key.
2. Hit CLX (reg). By hitting the yellow key, you move above the keys to the yellow level. In this case, you clear any information stored in the registers.
3. Hit the yellow key.
4. Hit X↔Y(fin). This clears the financial registers.

> Registers should always be cleared before using the calculator because, once information is stored, it stays stored until cleared.

Chapter 1

THE BORROWING OF MONEY

Outline
I. Simple Interest
    a. Exact interest/exact time
    b. Exact interest/ordinary time
    c. Ordinary interest/exact time
    d. Ordinary interest/ordinary time
II. *I = PRT*
    a. Finding rate
    b. Finding principal
    c. Finding time
III. Compound Interest
    a. Versus simple interest
    b. Continuous
IV. Add-on Interest
V. Annual Percentage Rate
    a. The Rule of 78
VI. Amortization
    a. Versus add-on interest

I. Simple Interest

To understand the borrowing of money, you must understand the formula $I = PRT$.

I refers to the interest (or finance charge).

P refers to the principal (or the amount of money borrowed).

R refers to the interest rate charged (it is very important to know the time period for which this rate is charged).

T refers to the length of time the money is borrowed.

Important: The units of time for the interest rate and the length of time borrowed are the same.

Example

You borrow $5,000 at 10% annual interest for six months:

$P = \$5,000$

$R = .10/\text{year}$

$T = .5 \text{ years}$

$I = (\$5,000)(.10/\text{year})(.5 \text{ years})$

$I = \$250$

In this example six months cannot be used if the interest rate is given on an annual basis.

Bankers and lenders have established guidelines for calculating simple interest using the following terms:

Exact interest. Refers to a 365-day year.

Ordinary interest. Refers to a 360-day year.

Exact time. Refers to counting the exact number of days between the date of loan and the due date.

Ordinary time. Refers to counting each month as having 30 days.

To calculate simple interest, you must count the number of days between two dates, by using either the calculator or the chart on page 3.

Example

Find the exact number of days between September 19, 1990 and June 19, 1991. First use the HP-12C calculator and then the chart.

Calculator Steps

1. Hit blue g key.
2. Hit 5(M DY). This establishes the date format that will be month, day, year.
3. Enter one or two digits for the month and then a period (9.).
4. Enter two digits for the day with no period following (19).
5. Enter four digits for the year (1990).
   The screen display should be 9.191990.
6. Hit ENTER.
7. Enter the second date using the same format as described above (6.191991).
8. Hit the blue g key; then hit EEX(DYS).
9. The answer should be 273.

Note: The calculator automatically takes care of leap years. If a leap year is involved, then the number of days in a year is 366.

Chart Steps   1. Find September 19 by going down the left-hand column to number 19 and across the row to the column labeled "Sept."

2. The number should be 262.

3. There are normally 365 days in a year. So, to find the number of days to the end of the year, subtract 262 from 365: 365 − 262 = 103.

4. Locate June 19 by the preceding method.

5. The number should be 170.

6. Adding 170 and 103 gives the total number of days between the two dates.

TABLE FOR THE EXACT NUMBER OF DAYS BETWEEN TWO DATES

Day of Month	Jan.	Feb.	Mar.	Apr.	May	June	July	Aug.	Sept.	Oct.	Nov.	Dec.
1	1	32	60	91	121	152	182	213	244	274	305	335
2	2	33	61	92	122	153	183	214	245	275	306	336
3	3	34	62	93	123	154	184	215	246	276	307	337
4	4	35	63	94	124	155	185	216	247	277	308	338
5	5	36	64	95	125	156	186	217	248	278	309	339
6	6	37	65	96	126	157	187	218	249	279	310	340
7	7	38	66	97	127	158	188	219	250	280	311	341
8	8	39	67	98	128	159	189	220	251	281	312	342
9	9	40	68	99	129	160	190	221	252	282	313	343
10	10	41	69	100	130	161	191	222	253	283	314	344
11	11	42	70	101	131	162	192	223	254	284	315	345
12	12	43	71	102	132	163	193	224	255	285	316	346
13	13	44	72	103	133	164	194	225	256	286	317	347
14	14	45	73	104	134	165	195	226	257	287	318	348
15	15	46	74	105	135	166	196	227	258	288	319	349
16	16	47	75	106	136	167	197	228	259	289	320	350
17	17	48	76	107	137	168	198	229	260	290	321	351
18	18	49	77	108	138	169	199	230	261	291	322	352
19	19	50	78	109	139	170	200	231	262	292	323	353
20	20	51	79	110	140	171	201	232	263	293	324	354
21	21	52	80	111	141	172	202	233	264	294	325	355
22	22	53	81	112	142	173	203	234	265	295	326	356
23	23	54	82	113	143	174	204	235	266	296	327	357
24	24	55	83	114	144	175	205	236	267	297	328	358
25	25	56	84	115	145	176	206	237	268	298	329	359
26	26	57	85	116	146	177	207	238	269	299	330	360
27	27	58	86	117	147	178	208	239	270	300	331	361
28	28	59	87	118	148	179	209	240	271	301	332	362
29	29	*	88	119	149	180	210	241	272	302	333	363
30	30		89	120	150	181	211	242	273	303	334	364
31	31		90		151		212	243		304		365

*Add one day for February 29 in leap years (1992, 1996, 2000, etc.).

The following examples illustrate how changing the words used on the loan document affects calculating interest.

Example 1

Pat wants to borrow $10,000 for six months. Today's date is August 10 and the due date is February 10. Calculate the interest owed on the loan if:

1. The rate is 12% exact interest at exact time:

$I = (\$10,000)(.12)(184/365)$

$I = \$604.93$

To calculate the exact number of days between August 10 and February 10, use the calculator or the chart on page 3.

2. The rate is 12% exact interest at ordinary time:

$I = (\$10,000)(.12)(180/365)$

$I = \$591.78$

3. The rate is 12% ordinary interest at exact time:

$I = (\$10,000)(.12)(184/360)$

$I = \$613.33$

4. The rate is 12% ordinary interest at ordinary time:

$I = (\$10,000)(.12)(180/360)$

$I = \$600.00$

Obviously, changing the words of a loan contract affects the amount of interest. Which loan method do you think most lending institutions prefer to use? (This is not a trick question.) You're right—number 3! Since the borrowing of money is normally in the form of a written contract, the parties to the contract should agree to (or at least understand) the terms of the contract.

II. *I = PRT*

As an investor, you should be able to calculate not only the interest but also the rate, principal, and time.

Example 1

You want to know how much money (principal) you need to invest to earn $3,000 at 12% ordinary interest at ordinary time over a period of six months. Rewrite the formula as follows:

$P = \dfrac{I}{(R)(T)}$

$P = \dfrac{\$3,000}{(.12)(180/360)}$

$P = \dfrac{3,000}{.06}$

$P = \$50,000$

Note: The time must be in the same units as the time period for the interest rate. Thus, we must convert days to years by dividing by 360.

> **Calculator Tip:** When using a calculator, calculate the denominator but do not round it off. Put this value into memory; then recall it when using it to finish the problem. Rounding off in the middle of calculations may lead to an error in the final answer. Rounding off should only be done after all calculations if possible. (Clear the calculator before doing the next problem.)

Calculator Steps

1. Enter .12, hit ENTER, hit 180, hit the TIMES key.
2. The value should be 21.6. Hit ENTER.
3. Enter 360; hit the DIVISION key.
4. The value should be .06.
5. Hit STO, and hit key 1. This stores the value in register one.
6. Enter 3000, hit ENTER, hit RCL, hit 1, hit the DIVISION key.
7. The value should be 50,000.

Example 2

Find the interest rate needed for $20,000 to earn $1,500 in six months' ordinary time, exact interest. Rewrite the formula as follows:

$$R = \frac{I}{(P)(T)}$$

$$R = \frac{1,500}{(20,000)(180/365)}$$

$$R = \frac{1,500}{9863.0137}$$

$$R = .15208$$

$$R = 15.21\%$$

Example 3

Find the time required for $8,000 to become $10,000 at 13.75% exact interest. Rewrite the formula as follows:

$$T = \frac{I}{(P)(R)}$$

$$T = \frac{2,000}{(8,000)(.1375)}$$

$$T = \frac{2,000}{1,100}$$

$$T = 1.8181818181 \text{ years}$$

To get an answer that makes sense, you must change the decimal part of the answer (.8181818181) into days or months. This can be accomplished by multiplying .8181818181 times the number of days in the year (in this case, 365).

Since (.8181818181)(365) rounds off to 299 days, it would take 1 year and 299 days for $8,000 to become $10,000 at 13.75% exact interest.

> **Note:** Interest rates are traditionally written as percentages on an annual basis. Most rates are carried out to two decimal places.

III. Compound Interest

The following examples demonstrate the difference between compound interest and simple interest.

Example 1

Calculate the simple interest on $10,000 at 12% for one year:

$I = PRT$

$I = (10,000)(.12)(1)$

$I = \$1,200$

At the end of one year, the bank account reads $11,200.

Example 2

Calculate the compound interest on $10,000 at 12% compounded quarterly for one year:

1. $I = (\$10,000)(.12)(.25)$
    $I = \$300$
2. $I = (\$10,300)(.12)(.25)$
    $I = \$309$
3. $I = (\$10,609)(.12)(.25)$
    $I = \$318.27$
4. $I = (\$10,927.27)(.12)(.25)$
    $I = \$327.82$

The total amount in the account at the end of one year is $11,255.09.

By simply changing the method of calculating the interest, the amount is increased by $55.09. Daily compounding would require 365 steps.

Calculator Steps

1. Enter 10,000, hit PV.
2. Enter 4, hit N. (Divide the rate by number of periods to get the rate per period, in this case 12 divided by 4 equals 3.)
3. Enter 3, hit i.
4. Hit FV.
5. The answer should be $11,255.09.

Now, to do this daily:

1. Hit 10,000, then PV.
2. Hit 365, then N.
3. Hit 12/365, then i.
4. Hit FV.
5. The answer should be $11,274.75.

Calculator Note: Most financial calculators are programmed to calculate compound interest.

IV. Add-on Interest

Add-on interest is the interest method used by most loan companies or installment plans.

Example

You want to purchase an item for $10,000 on an installment plan. The interest rate is 13% annually for a payback period of 5 years. To calculate the finance charge (interest), use:

$I = PRT$

$I = (10,000)(.13)(5)$

$I = \$6,500$

Calculate the monthly payment as follows:

$$\text{Monthly payment} = \frac{\text{Amount borrowed} + \text{Finance charge}}{\text{Total number of months}}$$

$$\text{Monthly payment} = \frac{\$10,000 + \$6,500}{60}$$

$$\text{Monthly payment} = \frac{\$16,500}{60}$$

$$\text{Monthly payment} = \$275.00$$

This procedure seems very straightforward, but let's check the annual percentage rate (APR) in the next section to see what is really happening.

V. Annual Percentage Rate

The *annual percentage rate (APR)* reflects the actual charge for money borrowed on an annual rate. In the preceding example, even though 13% was used to calculate the payment, the rate does not necessarily reflect the APR. By using the APR chart provided on pages 8 and 9, you can discover the actual APR. To do so, use the following formula:

$$\frac{\text{Finance charge}}{\text{Amount financed}} \times 100 = \text{Chart number}$$

Example

$$\frac{6,500}{10,000} \times 100 = 65$$

By using the left-hand column for 60 months, locate the number on the chart closest to the number 65. In this case, it is 64.86. This corresponds to an APR of 21.75%.

It is usually much easier to use the chart unless values cannot be found on the chart. If you cannot find the values by using the chart, use the formula for calculating APR:

$$APR = \frac{MF(95n + 9)}{12n(n + 1)(4P + F)}$$

M = number of payment periods in one year

F = total finance charge

n = total number of payments in the term of the loan

P = principal (amount borrowed)

Annual Percentage Rate

Finance Charge per $100 of Amount Financed

No. of Pmts.	2.00%	2.25%	2.50%	2.75%	3.00%	3.25%	3.50%	3.75%	4.00%	4.25%	4.50%	4.75%	5.00%	5.25%	5.50%	5.75%
6	$0.58	$0.66	$0.73	$0.80	$0.88	$0.95	$1.02	$1.10	$1.17	$1.24	$1.32	$1.39	$1.46	$1.54	$1.61	$1.68
12	1.09	1.22	1.36	1.50	1.63	1.77	1.91	2.04	2.18	2.32	2.45	2.59	2.73	2.87	3.00	3.14
18	1.59	1.79	1.99	2.19	2.39	2.59	2.79	2.99	3.20	3.40	3.60	3.80	4.00	4.21	4.41	4.61
24	2.10	2.36	2.62	2.89	3.15	3.42	3.69	3.95	4.22	4.49	4.75	5.02	5.29	5.56	5.83	6.10
30	2.60	2.93	3.26	3.59	3.92	4.25	4.58	4.92	5.25	5.58	5.92	6.25	6.59	6.92	7.26	7.60
36	3.11	3.51	3.90	4.30	4.69	5.09	5.49	5.89	6.29	6.69	7.09	7.49	7.90	8.30	8.71	9.11
42	3.62	4.08	4.54	5.00	5.47	5.93	6.40	6.86	7.33	7.80	8.27	8.74	9.21	9.69	10.16	10.64
48	4.14	4.66	5.19	5.72	6.24	6.78	7.31	7.84	8.38	8.92	9.46	10.00	10.54	11.09	11.63	12.18
54	4.65	5.24	5.83	6.43	7.03	7.63	8.23	8.83	9.44	10.04	10.65	11.26	11.88	12.49	13.11	13.73
60	5.17	5.82	6.48	7.15	7.81	8.48	9.15	9.82	10.50	11.18	11.86	12.54	13.23	13.92	14.61	15.30

Annual Percentage Rate

Finance Charge per $100 of Amount Financed

No. of Pmts.	6.00%	6.25%	6.50%	6.75%	7.00%	7.25%	7.50%	7.75%	8.00%	8.25%	8.50%	8.75%	9.00%	9.25%	9.50%	9.75%
6	$1.76	$1.83	$1.90	$1.98	$2.05	$2.13	$2.20	$2.27	$2.35	$2.42	$2.49	$2.57	$2.64	$2.72	$2.79	$2.86
12	3.28	3.42	3.56	3.69	3.83	3.97	4.11	4.25	4.39	4.52	4.66	4.80	4.94	5.08	5.22	5.36
18	4.82	5.02	5.22	5.43	5.63	5.84	6.04	6.25	6.45	6.66	6.86	7.07	7.28	7.48	7.69	7.90
24	6.37	6.64	6.91	7.18	7.45	7.73	8.00	8.27	8.55	8.82	9.09	9.37	9.64	9.92	10.19	10.47
30	7.94	8.28	8.61	8.96	9.30	9.64	9.98	10.32	10.66	11.01	11.35	11.70	12.04	12.39	12.74	13.09
36	9.52	9.93	10.34	10.75	11.16	11.57	11.98	12.40	12.81	13.23	13.64	14.06	14.48	14.90	15.32	15.74
42	11.12	11.60	12.08	12.56	13.04	13.52	14.01	14.50	14.98	15.47	15.96	16.45	16.95	17.44	17.94	18.43
48	12.73	13.28	13.83	14.39	14.94	15.50	16.06	16.62	17.18	17.75	18.31	18.88	19.45	20.02	20.59	21.16
54	14.36	14.98	15.61	16.23	16.86	17.50	18.13	18.77	19.41	20.05	20.69	21.34	21.98	22.63	23.28	23.94
60	16.00	16.70	17.40	18.10	18.81	19.52	20.23	20.94	21.66	22.38	23.10	23.82	24.55	25.28	26.01	26.75

Annual Percentage Rate

Finance Charge per $100 of Amount Financed

No. of Pmts.	10.00%	10.25%	10.50%	10.75%	11.00%	11.25%	11.50%	11.75%	12.00%	12.25%	12.50%	12.75%	13.00%	13.25%	13.50%	13.75%
6	$ 2.94	$ 3.01	$ 3.08	$ 3.16	$ 3.23	$ 3.31	$ 3.38	$ 3.45	$ 3.53	$ 3.60	$ 3.68	$ 3.75	$ 3.83	$ 3.90	$ 3.97	$ 4.05
12	5.50	5.64	5.78	5.92	6.06	6.20	6.34	6.48	6.62	6.76	6.90	7.04	7.18	7.32	7.46	7.60
18	8.10	8.31	8.52	8.73	8.93	9.14	9.35	9.56	9.77	9.98	10.19	10.40	10.61	10.82	11.03	11.24
24	10.75	11.02	11.30	11.58	11.86	12.14	12.42	12.70	12.98	13.26	13.54	13.82	14.10	14.38	14.66	14.95
30	13.43	13.78	14.13	14.48	14.83	15.19	15.54	15.89	16.24	16.60	16.95	17.31	17.66	18.02	18.38	18.74
36	16.16	16.58	17.01	17.43	17.86	18.29	18.71	19.14	19.57	20.00	20.43	20.87	21.30	21.73	22.17	22.60
42	18.93	19.43	19.93	20.43	20.93	21.44	21.94	22.45	22.96	23.47	23.98	24.49	25.00	25.51	26.03	26.55
48	21.74	22.32	22.90	23.48	24.06	24.64	25.23	25.81	26.40	26.99	27.58	28.18	28.77	29.37	29.97	30.57
54	24.59	25.25	25.91	26.57	27.23	27.90	28.56	29.23	29.91	30.58	31.25	31.93	32.61	33.29	33.98	34.66
60	27.48	28.22	28.96	29.71	30.45	31.20	31.96	32.71	33.47	34.23	34.99	35.75	36.52	37.29	38.06	38.83

SOURCE: Walter H. Lange and Temoleon G. Rousos, *Business and Consumer Mathematics*, 5th ed. (Irwin: Homewood, IL, 1992).

Annual Percentage Rate

Finance Charge per $100 of Amount Financed

No. of Pmts.	14.00%	14.25%	14.50%	14.75%	15.00%	15.25%	15.50%	15.75%	16.00%	16.25%	16.50%	16.75%	17.00%	17.25%	17.50%	17.75%
6	$ 4.12	$ 4.20	$ 4.27	$ 4.35	$ 4.42	$ 4.49	$ 4.57	$ 4.64	$ 4.72	$ 4.79	$ 4.87	$ 4.94	$ 5.02	$ 5.09	$ 5.17	$ 5.24
12	7.72	7.89	8.03	8.17	8.31	8.45	8.59	8.74	8.88	9.02	9.16	9.30	9.45	9.59	9.73	9.87
18	11.45	11.66	11.87	12.08	12.29	12.50	12.72	12.93	13.14	13.35	13.57	13.78	13.99	14.21	14.42	14.64
24	15.23	15.51	15.80	16.08	16.37	16.65	16.94	17.22	17.51	17.80	18.09	18.37	18.66	18.95	19.24	19.53
30	19.10	19.45	19.81	20.17	20.54	20.90	21.26	21.62	21.99	22.35	22.72	23.08	23.45	23.81	24.18	24.55
36	23.04	23.48	23.92	24.35	24.80	25.24	25.68	26.12	26.57	27.01	27.46	27.90	28.35	28.80	29.25	29.70
42	27.06	27.58	28.10	28.62	29.15	29.67	30.19	30.72	31.25	31.78	32.31	32.84	33.37	33.90	34.44	34.97
48	31.17	31.77	32.37	32.98	33.59	34.20	34.81	35.42	36.03	36.65	37.27	37.88	38.50	39.13	39.75	40.37
54	35.35	36.04	36.73	37.42	38.12	38.82	39.52	40.22	40.92	41.63	42.33	43.04	43.75	44.47	45.18	45.90
60	39.61	40.39	41.17	41.95	42.74	43.53	44.32	45.11	45.91	46.71	47.51	48.31	49.12	49.92	50.73	51.55

Annual Percentage Rate

Finance Charge per $100 of Amount Financed

No. of Pmts.	18.00%	18.25%	18.50%	18.75%	19.00%	19.25%	19.50%	19.75%	20.00%	20.25%	20.50%	20.75%	21.00%	21.25%	21.50%	21.75%
6	$ 5.32	$ 5.39	$ 5.46	$ 5.54	$ 5.61	$ 5.69	$ 5.76	$ 5.84	$ 5.91	$ 5.99	$ 6.06	$ 6.14	$ 6.21	$ 6.29	$ 6.36	$ 6.44
12	10.02	10.16	10.30	10.44	10.59	10.73	10.87	11.02	11.16	11.31	11.45	11.59	11.74	11.88	12.02	12.17
18	14.85	15.07	15.28	15.49	15.71	15.93	16.14	16.36	16.57	16.79	17.01	17.22	17.44	17.66	17.88	18.09
24	19.82	20.11	20.40	20.69	20.98	21.27	21.56	21.86	22.15	22.44	22.74	23.03	23.33	23.62	23.92	24.21
30	24.92	25.29	25.66	26.03	26.40	26.77	27.14	27.52	27.89	28.26	28.64	29.01	29.39	29.77	30.14	30.52
36	30.15	30.60	31.05	31.51	31.96	32.42	32.87	33.33	33.79	34.25	34.71	35.17	35.63	36.09	36.56	37.02
42	35.51	36.05	36.59	37.13	37.67	38.21	38.76	39.30	39.85	40.40	40.95	41.50	42.05	42.60	43.15	43.71
48	41.00	41.63	42.26	42.89	43.52	44.15	44.79	45.43	46.07	46.71	47.35	47.99	48.64	49.28	49.93	50.58
54	46.62	47.34	48.06	48.79	49.51	50.24	50.97	51.70	52.44	53.17	53.91	54.65	55.39	56.14	56.88	57.63
60	52.36	53.18	54.00	54.82	55.64	56.47	57.30	58.13	58.96	59.80	60.64	61.48	62.32	63.17	64.01	64.86

Annual Percentage Rate

Finance Charge per $100 of Amount Financed

No. of Pmts.	22.00%	22.25%	22.50%	22.75%	23.00%	23.25%	23.50%	23.75%	24.00%	24.25%	24.50%	24.75%	25.00%	25.25%	25.50%	25.75%
6	$ 6.51	$ 6.59	$ 6.66	$ 6.74	$ 6.81	$ 6.89	$ 6.96	$ 7.04	$ 7.12	$ 7.19	$ 7.27	$ 7.34	$ 7.42	$ 7.49	$ 7.57	$ 7.64
12	12.31	12.46	12.60	12.75	12.89	13.04	13.18	13.33	13.47	13.62	13.76	13.91	14.05	14.20	14.34	14.49
18	18.31	18.53	18.75	18.97	19.19	19.41	19.62	19.84	20.06	20.28	20.50	20.72	20.95	21.17	21.39	21.61
24	24.51	24.80	25.10	25.40	25.70	25.99	26.29	26.59	26.89	27.19	27.49	27.79	28.09	28.39	28.69	29.00
30	30.90	31.28	31.66	32.04	32.42	32.80	33.18	33.57	33.95	34.33	34.72	35.10	35.49	35.88	36.26	36.65
36	37.49	37.95	38.42	38.89	39.35	39.82	40.29	40.77	41.24	41.71	42.19	42.66	43.14	43.61	44.09	44.57
42	44.26	44.82	45.38	45.94	46.50	47.06	47.62	48.19	48.75	49.32	49.89	50.46	51.03	51.60	52.17	52.74
48	51.23	51.88	52.54	53.19	53.85	54.51	55.16	55.83	56.49	57.15	57.82	58.49	59.15	59.82	60.50	61.17
54	58.33	59.13	59.88	60.65	61.40	62.16	62.92	63.68	64.44	65.21	65.98	66.75	67.52	68.29	69.07	69.84
60	65.71	66.57	67.42	68.28	69.14	70.01	70.87	71.74	72.61	73.48	74.35	75.23	76.11	76.99	77.87	78.76

SOURCE: Walter H. Lange and Temoleon G. Rousos, *Business and Consumer Mathematics*, 5th ed. (Irwin: Homewood, IL, 1992).

The Rule of 78

If you find yourself in a contract of add-on interest and you would like to pay it off, you are about to find another very unpleasant fact about this type of loan.

Most of these contracts use the Rule of 78 for early payoffs. While the rule is used to give a refund on interest due, in most cases you will pay much more interest for the borrowed money than expected.

The number 78 comes about by adding the numbers from 1 to 12, the number of months in a year. If the rule is used over a two-year period, it would be the Rule of 300, which represents the sum of the numbers from 1 to 24.

> ### *Example*
>
> You borrow $2,000 at 12% for one year. For this example, dispense with using the concepts of ordinary or exact interest.
>
> $I = PRT$
>
> $I = (2,000)(.12)(1)$
>
> $I = 240$
>
> Then calculate the monthly payment:
>
> $\dfrac{\$2,000 + 240}{12} = \$186.67$
>
> The APR:
>
> $\dfrac{240}{2,000} \times 100 = 12$ yields 21.5%

After reviewing the APR, the borrower decides to pay off the loan with the fifth payment. In order to calculate the *refund fraction,* we need to introduce a simple mathematical formula for calculating sums of consecutive numbers.

$$S = \frac{N(N+1)}{2}$$

This formula gives the total of all whole numbers from 1 to N.

Try it on the sum of the numbers from 1 to 12, since we know the answer is 78:

$$S = \frac{12(12 + 1)}{2}$$

$$S = \frac{12(13)}{2}$$

$$S = \frac{156}{2}$$

$$S = 78$$

To calculate the refund fraction, calculate a numerator and a denominator. The denominator is always the sum of the total number of payments. The numerator is the sum of the number of payments that remain.

Example

The total number of payments is 12; therefore, the denominator is 78. Seven payments are left after the fifth payment is made. Therefore:

$S = \dfrac{7(8)}{2}$

$S = \dfrac{56}{2}$

$S = 28$

The refund fraction then becomes 28/78. This is the fraction of the total amount of finance charge that is to be refunded to you for paying the loan off early.

Example

To calculate this refund, multiply the refund fraction times the total finance charge:

$\dfrac{28}{78} \times 240 = \$86.15$

To figure your payoff:

Add the 4 payments of $186.67 already made. This equals $746.68.

The total for all payments is $2,240. Therefore subtract $746.68 from $2,240:

$$\begin{aligned}
&\$2,240.00 \\
-\ &\$\underline{\quad746.68} \\
&\$1,493.32
\end{aligned}$$

Then subtract the refund of $86.15:

$$\begin{aligned}
&\$1,493.32 \\
-\ &\$\underline{\quad\ 86.15}
\end{aligned}$$

Payoff amount due: $1,407.17

This looks like a fair deal until you take a look at how much interest you paid to borrow money for five months:

Total interest	$240.00
Less refund:	– $ 86.15
Interest paid for five months	$153.85

The common-sense approach would be to pay less than $120 since the money was used for less than six months, but this is not the way the Rule of 78 works. The lending institution justifies the Rule of 78 by saying that, since you owed more money in the beginning, you should have paid more interest. This leads us into a comparison of add-on interest versus mortgage money.

VI. Amortization

Review the following examples:

Example 1

$10,000 at 13% for 5 years add-on interest

$I = (\$10,000)(.13)(5)$

$I = \$6,500$

Monthly payment = $\dfrac{\$10,000 + \$6,500}{60}$

Monthly payment = $275.00

Find the APR

$\dfrac{\$6,500}{\$10,000} \times 100 = 65$ From the chart (or formula) the APR is 21.75%

Example 2

$10,000 at 13% amortized over 5 years

To calculate the monthly payment of an amortized loan, use the following formula:

$$P_n = L \left[\dfrac{i}{1 - \dfrac{1}{(1 + i)^n}} \right]$$

P_n = payment

L = amount borrowed

I = yearly interest rate

n = number of payments

Thank goodness for financial calculators! Wouldn't it be fun to have to figure your mortgage payment by using this formula?

Almost all financial calculators have the following keys:

PMT = payment

n = number of payments

i = interest rate per period

PV = present value (amount borrowed)

We will spend much time in Chapter 3 becoming experts in the use of these keys.

Calculator Steps to Find Mortgage Payment

1. Enter 10,000, then hit PV.
2. Enter 13, hit blue g, then hit i.
3. Enter 5, hit blue g, then hit n.
4. Hit PMT.
5. The payment should be –$227.53.

1. If you are using an HP-12C, your payment will have a negative sign in front of it. No need to panic. This is HP's way of telling you that it is a payment.

2. If using a calculator other than an HP-12C, understand that when the blue g key is used it automatically divides by 12 or multiplies by 12. (The most used time period for mortgages is the month.) If a different time frame were to be used, then the actual division and multiplication would have to be done. We will examine this in Chapter 3.

To find the finance charge on the mortgage payment:

Example

Multiply 60 times the payment and subtract the amount borrowed:

$(60)(227.53) = \$13{,}651.80$

$$\begin{aligned} &\$13{,}651.80 \\ -\ &\underline{\$10{,}000.00} \\ &\$\ 3{,}651.80 \end{aligned}$$

To find the APR:

$$\frac{\$3{,}651.80}{\$10{,}000} \times 100 = 36.518$$

By using the APR chart or formula, you find that the APR is exactly 13%.

Why does this method of payment have an actual APR the same as the rate you are being charged to borrow the money?
Because mortgage interest rates are true annual percentage rates!

Let us analyze the first three monthly payments of this mortgage. The interest charged in this payment is calculated the way all interest is calculated—by using the formula $I = PRT$. You must therefore understand:

- how much money is being borrowed;
- for what interest rate; and
- most important, over what time period.

Example

Since the payment is being made at the end of the first month, you have borrowed \$10,000 for exactly one month at 13%. Therefore, calculate the interest owed as follows:

$I = (\$10{,}000)(.13)(1/12)$

$I = \$108.33$

Since your payment was \$227.53, the excess over \$108.33 goes toward paying off the amount borrowed (\$10,000). This excess is calculated by subtracting \$108.33 from \$227.53 = \$119.20, which is paid toward the mortgage. At the end of one month the following changes have occurred:

1. $108.33 in interest was paid for using $10,000 for one month.

2. The new amount owed is:

$10,000.00
− $ 119.20
$ 9,880.80

For the next month you will borrow $9,880.20 at 13%. Your payment remains the same, but the amount you pay in interest will be lowered since you have borrowed less money and the amount going toward reducing the loan will be increased. The same steps are used to compute the interest and new balance:

$I = (\$9,880.80)(.13)(1/12)$

$I = \$107.04$

$227.53
− $107.04
$120.49

This represents the amount paid toward the amount borrowed.

$9,980.20
− $ 120.49
$9,760.31

Most homeowners are used to seeing a bank statement at the end of the year that reflects the amount of interest paid and the new balance on the loan. The key fact to remember on an amortized loan is that you pay interest only on the remaining balance at the end of each payment. Also, with most mortgages there is no prepayment penalty, no Rule of 78. Therefore, when you pay off your loan, what you see is what you owe. The following chart represents an amortization schedule on the preceding loan for one year.

Payment #	Payment	Interest	Principal	Balance
1	$ 227.53	$ 108.33	$ 119.20	$9,880.80
2	$ 227.53	$ 107.04	$ 120.49	$9,760.31
3	$ 227.53	$ 105.74	$ 121.79	$9,638.52
4	$ 227.53	$ 104.42	$ 123.11	$9,515.41
5	$ 227.53	$ 103.08	$ 124.45	$9,390.96
6	$ 227.53	$ 101.74	$ 125.79	$9,265.17
7	$ 227.53	$ 100.37	$ 127.16	$9,138.01
8	$ 227.53	$ 99.00	$ 128.53	$9,009.48
9	$ 227.53	$ 97.60	$ 129.93	$8,879.55
10	$ 227.53	$ 96.20	$ 131.33	$8,748.22
11	$ 227.53	$ 94.77	$ 132.76	$8,615.46
12	$ 227.53	$ 93.33	$ 134.20	$8,481.26
Totals:	$2,730.36	$1,211.62	$1,518.74	

The total amount paid this year is:	$2,730.36
The total amount of interest paid for this year is:	$1,211.62
The total amount of principal paid this year is:	$1,518.74
The new balance at the end of this year is:	$8,481.26

Summary

Anyone who wishes to borrow money must understand how it is to be paid back. Using the information in this chapter, an investor can see that the best way to borrow money is in the form of a mortgage.

PROBLEM SET 1

1. A sporting goods company invested money at 13.5% ordinary interest. It earned $70 in 30 days. How much money was invested?

2. Willie would like to establish a savings account paying him $150 every 30 days. What principal would he require if he can invest it at 8.5% exact interest?

3. A bank pays interest quarterly. At the end of the first quarter, it paid $23.28 on an account containing $1,898. What is the rate of interest?

4. PP&L charged a late fee of $6.84 on an electric bill for $130.80, which was 10 days late. What exact interest rate is being charged?

5. John Paul deposited $8,700 at 9.5% ordinary interest and earned $239.28. How many days was the money deposited?

6. Julia borrowed $1,550 at 12.5% exact interest to pay her tuition. On the due date, she paid the bank $1,581.03. What was the term of the loan (to the nearest day)?

7. An '84 Subaru costing $3,795 is financed at ABC Credit Corporation at 10.21% add-on interest for 24 months with a down payment of $755. Find the:

   a. amount financed.

   b. finance charge.

   c. total amount paid in installments.

   d. monthly payments.

   e. annual percentage rate.

8. A Mustang costing $7,588 was purchased for $2,588 down, and the remainder was financed with a 36-month loan at 9% add-on interest. The finance charge was $1,350. Monthly payments were $176.39. The buyer decided to pay off the loan at the end of one year (with the 12th payment).

   a. Under the Rule of 78, determine the amount of the final payment.

   b. Calculate the total amount of interest paid.

9. Jane purchased $6,400 worth of furniture by making a $3,400 down payment and signing a note for the remaining $3,000. The note called for 15 monthly payments of $225 (a finance charge of $375). If Jane decides to pay off the note with her sixth payment and the Rule of 78 applies, find:

   a. the amount of the final payment.

   b. the total amount of interest paid.

10. A Buick costing $15,968 is purchased by putting down $1,250 and financing the balance at 9.5% add-on interest for 3 years. Find the:

   a. amount financed.

   b. finance charge.

   c. total amount paid in installments.

   d. monthly payment.

   e. annual percentage rate.

   f. final payment if paid off with 15th payment (Rule of 78 applies) and total amount of interest paid.

Chapter 2

Risk versus Return: How to Decide When to Invest

Outline

I. Risks

    a. The list of reasons why people are afraid to invest

II. Returns

    a. The list of reasons why people invest anyhow

    b. Cash flow concepts

    c. Introduction to methods for property evaluation

I. Risks

First we should define some terms to make sure we understand what it is we are talking about.

Invest: To put out money, time, or whatever to receive a benefit or reward.

Return: The benefit or reward received.

Risk: The possibility of not getting the reward after putting out the money, time, or whatever.

Most investors are looking for a way to maximize their wealth. They would like to do this in the easiest and least complicated way possible. The direction many investors prefer is the stock market. Many consider the stock market to be perfect because:

1. Information is readily available to the public.
2. The price and quantity of stocks are reported immediately.
3. It is easy to transfer shares.
4. Stocks are usually easy to liquidate.
5. The market is well organized and centralized.
6. The market adjusts quickly to supply and demand.
7. Stock is easy to obtain through many conduits.
8. The market offers the ability to sell short or gamble in commodities and options.

All of these nice, clean characteristics are available to you, the buyer, as long as you qualify, and as long as you have the cash.

The real estate market does not measure up to the standards of the stock market. But, because it is not such a perfect market, real estate offers opportunity to all who are short on cash but high on creativity. The characteristics of the real estate market that intrigue investors are:

1. **Leverage.**
2. Sheriff sales.
3. Divorces.
4. Forced liquidation.
5. **Leverage.**
6. Transfers.
7. Management headaches.
8. Tax concerns.
9. Rezoning possibilities.
10. **Leverage.**

Obviously, the biggest single item that causes the investor to buy real estate is leverage. One of the secrets to increasing your return is to use less of your money and more of someone else's.

Still, all people who consider investing understand that risks are involved. Here are some of the risks:

1. The number one fear of most people is of the *loss of their principal investment.* Most people would prefer to have an investment that is insured or guaranteed. The trouble with this kind of investment is that the return is low.

2. Buying an investment property always brings up the possibility of the *loss of income.* Many times a property may be advertised with "potential" rent (or rents are too low) and this just isn't the case. Investors usually look at worst-case scenarios before buying. Some investments, such as land, have no income and depend solely on appreciation or inflation.

3. *When to buy* is a concern of all investors. No one knows what is going to happen tomorrow. Depending on inflation or increase in demand is definitely a risk.

4. *Converting the property to cash* in a down market may be very difficult. Learning how to borrow against your property becomes extremely important. Location becomes vital. You should always ask yourself the following question before a purchase: "Could I sell this property tomorrow and get back the price I'm paying for it today?" If the answer to this question is no, then buying it may be a serious mistake.

5. Most properties are not affected by *deflation,* but it is always a possibility that a property could be purchased and go down in value. This kind of deflation affected Midwest farmers during the early 1980s when property values dropped as much as 21%.

6. Some people are not cut out for the *management* of property, and they either cannot afford to have a manager or feel a manager is unnecessary. Some of these people would love to invest but have a problem with someone else managing their investment.

Probably many other reasons could prevent a potential investor from buying, but it is the willingness to accept possible risks that warrants the lucrative returns on investment properties.

II. Returns

With respect to returns, several guidelines should be established so that all investors have a consistent procedure for determining their return. Here are some fundamentals when discussing returns:

1. *All returns should be expressed in the form of a percentage on an annual basis.* Returns should not be expressed in the form of dollars. A $1,000 return is terrific if you invested $5,000 for the year (a 20% return), but not if you invested $100,000 (a 1% return).
2. *Understand what you are basing your return on.* If you purchase a $100,000 property and put $20,000 down, do you calculate your return on your investment of $20,000? What about your closing costs? What about the fact that it took a year for the money to be returned? What about appreciation? What about principal reduction from the mortgage payment? Returns should be based on the total equity in the property at the time of calculating the return.
3. *All returns should be stated after taxes.* Many times people talk about the return they are getting on a CD or some other investment prior to these returns being affected by tax consequences. Compare any investment vehicle returns after taxes.

Returns from investment properties fall into four categories:

1. *Cash flows:* This is the amount of money left after all the expenses and mortgage payments have been made. The two types of cash flows are:
   a. Before-tax cash flow.
   b. After-tax cash flow.
2. *Appreciation:* This is the increase in the value of the property over the original cost while the property is owned. This cash flow is difficult to project and usually is determined only by the sale of the property. It becomes important for an investor to buy in areas that traditionally have increased in property value.
3. *Principal reduction:* This is the the amount of money from your mortgage payment that reduces the money borrowed to purchase the property. It is as if you are making an additional down payment with each payment. Some investors choose to make interest-only payments and not invest any other money than their original down payment. Remember that the interest part of the payment is an expense.

4. *Tax shelter:* This refers to the tax savings that can occur from owning an investment property. Many interesting concepts—such as depreciation, installment sales, tax-deferred exchanges, etc.—can save an investor money with regard to taxes. *Remember: You can only enjoy the benefit of a tax shelter if you owe taxes.* The government does not just give you money because your investment lost money on paper. What you're able to do is keep more of the money that you have earned. Note the following:

   a. Income taxes do not affect cash flow before taxes, appreciation, or principal reduction.

   b. Depreciation is strange because it is not an actual out-of-pocket cash expense. It is a computed expense to be deducted only for income tax purposes. More time will be spent later on depreciation, but since the Tax Reform Bill of 1986 all depreciation is calculated on a straight-line basis. This means that if the useful life of a property is 27.5 years and the value of the improvement (you cannot depreciate the land) is $275,000, then you receive a paper loss of $10,000 per year.

   c. If a property shows a loss, it may be deducted from other income (the IRS establishes the limit that may be deducted). It is imperative that you contact a knowledgeable accountant to be assured of how the purchase and ownership of a property affects your taxes.

After reviewing risks and returns, you need to examine several vital areas:

1. Every investor's *objectives, goals,* and *constraints* should be identified. Not every investor is interested in cash flow. The realtor or investor must find out this information to properly search for property that meets the investor's needs.

2. Investors should hold *ownership* in any property in a way that legally benefits them the most. Several possibilities are to own the property as an individual, partnership, or corporation. Your accountant and attorney should help you make this decision.

3. Have a working knowledge of the *lending institutions* in the area where you intend to buy. This determines your ability to purchase the property in most cases. Take a banker to lunch!

4. Know the *zoning* restrictions that apply to any areas you are interested in. Each local municipality makes available to the public its zoning regulations and zoning maps.

5. Understand the *rights of the tenant* to whom you will be renting. Many states have a Landlord-Tenant Act that spells out the rights of the landlord and the tenant. Develop a strong screening process that could prevent problems. Know what your lease says. *Don't just sign a standardized piece of paper. Read it!*

6. Develop an understanding of *the market.* What is the present supply and demand? Should the investment be in residential, industrial, or commercial property? Where is the property located? Get information on the demographics of the area.

7. Understand the *tax ramifications* of purchasing an investment property. Realtors are not expert accountants. Their job is to find investors what they are looking for. No realtor should ever be giving advice regarding taxes!

Once you locate a property, the next step is to analyze it to see if it meets your cash flow criteria. The remainder of this book is going to take a look at how to collect and analyze the data that will help you make the best decision in buying an investment property. That decision is based on:

1. Collecting the annual property operating data.
2. Calculating the before- and after-tax cash flows.
3. Calculating the cash flow from the sale of the property.
4. Calculating the internal rate of return.

Before we start using this decision-making process for purchasing an investment property, let us look at a couple of rules of thumb commonly used to calculate the value of property.

The Appraisal

An appraisal actually entails three appraisals:

1. The *sales comparison approach* establishes a price by comparing other similar properties that have sold within the past year.
2. The *cost approach* establishes a price if the property were to be rebuilt at today's prices.
3. The *income approach* establishes a price by using the gross income multiplier to calculate what the property would rent for in a particular neighborhood.

The gross income multiplier is:

$$\text{GIM} = \frac{\text{Value (selling price)}}{\text{Gross yearly income}}$$

If the GIM for a particular area is known, then the selling price of a property can be found by using:

$$\text{Value (selling price)} = (\text{GIM}) \times \text{Gross yearly income}$$

For an investment property, most weight is usually given to the income approach. The problem with this method is that most areas do not have established GIMs. The problem becomes very obvious when a property is owned in a neighborhood with a college. Here, a two-unit property might rent to college students for $1,000 per month while the place next door without college students rents for only $600. No two properties are alike and, to investors, this becomes even more apparent.

Capitalization Rate

This seems to be a very common tool for establishing price by most realtors. They find a number that they call the *capitalization rate* and use it to determine list price of the property. The formula for capitalization rate is:

Capitalization rate = $\dfrac{\text{Net operating income}}{\text{Value (selling price)}}$

Therefore,

Value (selling price) = $\dfrac{\text{Net operating income}}{\text{Capitalization rate}}$

This is very convenient, but how do you come up with the capitalization rate? Most investors would agree that the capitalization rate is established by them, not by the property and its net operating income. This number becomes inconsistent because it is different for every investor. There is no set capitalization rate for an area.

Some people use a technique called the *band of investment.* This establishes a capitalization rate by adding three different percentages:

- The return of investment.
- The return on a low risk or safe investment.
- The return for the added risk on this investment.

The *return of investment* is calculated by determining how long the investor thinks it will take to recoup the initial investment.

> **Example:**
>
> The investor feels it will take 25 years. This percent is 1/25 or 4%. If a safe investment at the bank is 5.25%, then the total so far is 9.25%. Now comes the kicker: How much extra return do you want for taking additional risk? If you feel that you need an additional 5%, you have just established your capitalization rate at 14.25%.
>
> If a property is on the market for $200,000 and has a net operating income of $20,000, by using your "cap" rate, you can determine what you feel the property is worth:
>
> Value (selling price) = $\dfrac{\$20,000}{.1425}$
>
> Value (selling price) = $140,350.88
>
> Now there's an interesting offer!

To get a general feel for cash flows and the effect of taxes, use the following procedures to answer the problems at the end of the chapter. The formats are not specific to individual situations, but give you an outline as to how certain values are arrived at, particularly by the Internal Revenue Service. Later, these procedures will be incorporated into an easy-to-fill-in form.

How to Find After-Tax Cash Flows Each Year

Take the *scheduled rental income*
  (Less vacancy and bad debts)
  Plus miscellaneous income
Equals *gross operating income*
  (Less operating expenses)
Equals *net operating income*
  (Less debt service)
Equals *before-tax cash flow*
  [Less taxes (or plus if tax savings)]*
Equals *after-tax cash flow*

* Must use the step below to calculate this number.

How to Find Taxes from Operation for Each Year

Take *gross operating income*
  (Less operating expenses)
Equals *net operating income*
  (Less interest on debt)
  (Less depreciation)
Equals *ordinary taxable Income*
  Times investor's marginal tax rate
Equals *taxes (or tax savings)*

How to Calculate Net Proceeds from Sale of an Investment

Take *expected selling price*
  (Less selling expenses)
  (Less mortgage balances)
Equals *proceeds before taxes*
  (Less taxes due on sale) *
Equals *net proceeds after taxes*

* Must use the step below to calculate this number.

How to Calculate Taxes Due on Sale of an Investment

Take *original basis (purchase price)*
  Plus capital improvements
  Plus selling expenses
  (Less accumulated depreciation)
  (Less partial sales)
Equals *adjusted cost basis*
Take *sale price*
  (Less adjusted cost basis)
Equals *taxable gain on sale*
  Times investor's tax rate
Equals *taxes due on sale*

PROBLEM SET 2

1. A real estate investment has the following inputs:
   a. Asking price $450,000
   b. Rentable area   8,500 square feet
   c. Rent per square foot $10 per year
   d. Vacancy losses   7% per year
   e. Operating expenses $22,000
   f. Debt service $43,187, of which $35,696 is interest
   g. Depreciation deduction $14,545
   h. Investor's marginal tax rate   30%
   Compute the expected after-tax cash flow from operation for year one.

2. You have recently sold your apartment building for $500,000. It was purchased for $400,000 five years ago. You have taken depreciation deductions of $18,000 per year. The unpaid mortgage balance is $325,000. Your income tax rate on ordinary income is 30%. Total selling expenses are 6% of sale price. Capital improvements costs are $48,000. Compute your net sales proceeds after taxes.

3. Using the information in Problem 1, compute the following:
   a. Gross income multiplier: $\text{GIM} = \dfrac{\text{Value}}{\text{Gross yearly income}}$
   b. Capitalization rate: $\text{Cap Rate} = \dfrac{\text{Net operating income}}{\text{Value}}$

4. Using the facts from Problem 1, suppose the appropriate overall capitalization rate was 10.5%. What is the indicated value of the property using the estimated net operating income?

5. Andrew is considering buying an apartment house. Consider the following information:

Asking price	$165,000
Down payment	$ 25,000
Balance on contract at 8%	
(Annual payment $15,000)	$140,000
Land value	$ 30,000
Improvements	$135,000
Life for depreciation	27.5 years
Investor's tax bracket	30%
Income Statement	
Annual income after vacancies	$ 30,000
Expenses:	
Real estate taxes	$ 3,250
Mortgage payment	$ 15,000
Maintenance and repair	$ 2,000
Management	$ 2,000
Utilities	$ 3,000

    a. Based on a gross income multiplier of 7, the indicated value of the property is how much?

    b. The first-year interest expense will be *approximately* how much?

    c. Operating expenses for this apartment building should be how much?

    d. The net operating income for this property should be *approximately* how much?

    e. The cash flow before income tax will be how much?

    f. Taxable income is how much?

    g. At a 4% appreciation rate, the apartment building will be worth how much in one year?

6. For a property with a net operating income of $12,000, what would be the value if the investor desires a rate of return of

    a. 8%?

    b. 11%?

    c. 20%?

7. A property had a net operating income of $8,500. If it sold for the following prices, what would be the capitalization rate?

    a. $100,000

    b. $64,000

    c. $88,000

8. If a property sold for $85,000 and the following capitalization rates were used, what was the net operating income in each case?

    a. 8.5%

    b. 10%

    c. 12%

9. Sarah is interested in buying a property that had a $10,000 net operating income. With money in the bank earning 3.7% interest, Sarah is willing to withdraw it if at least 6% additional income could be realized for the risk of withdrawing it. Sarah felt it would take 40 years to get her return of investment.

    a. What capitalization rate should this investor use to capitalize the $10,000?

    b. What could the investor pay for the property based on this capitalization rate?

Chapter 3

USING THE FINANCIAL CALCULATOR

Outline

I. General use of the calculator to find FV, PV, i, n, and PMT

II. Calculating mortgage payments, remaining balances, accumulated interest, and principal reduction.

Remember: Your calculator's financial registers should be cleared prior to the start of each problem by hitting the yellow f key, then keys CLX (Reg) and X↔Y (Fin).

I. General Use of the Calculator to Find FV, PV, i, n, and PMT

This chapter is written specifically for the use of the Hewlett-Packard 12C financial calculator, primarily through sample questions.

Note: To set the number of decimal places on your screen, hit the yellow f key, then the desired number of places. Since the majority of problems deal with money, we use two places. Therefore, hit the yellow f key, then 2.

Example 1

What is the monthly mortgage payment on a $20,000 mortgage to be amortized over 20 years at 8%?

Calculator Steps

1. Enter 20,000, hit PV.
2. Enter 8, hit blue g key, hit i.
3. Enter 20, hit blue g key, hit n.
4. Hit PMT, to receive an answer of $167.29.

Note: Your answer is a negative because the HP-12C indicates this is a payout.

Example 2

Find the remaining balance on the preceding problem after 3 years. Remember to *clear registers*.

Calculator Steps

1. Enter 20,000, hit PV.
2. Enter 167.29, hit CHS, hit PMT.
3. Enter 8, hit blue g key, hit i.
4. Enter 36 (the number of monthly payments made over a 3-year period).
5. Hit the yellow f key, hit n. (By hitting the yellow f key, you actually perform the function above the n key, which in this case is amort, referring to amortizing.)
6. This should give the value **–4,646.00** (the *total interest paid* for the last 36 payments).
7. Hit the X↔Y key.
8. This should give the value **–1,376.44** (the *principal reduction* for the last 36 payments).
9. Hit RCL, then PV.
10. This should give the value **18,623.55** (the *remaining balance* after the last 36 payments).

Don't clear that calculator yet!

Suppose someone asks you to find the balance after five years. The HP-12C has in its memory all the information for the last 36 months. All you need to do is to find the balance after the next 24 months.

Calculator Steps

1. Enter 24, hit the yellow f key, then the n (amort) key.
2. The value should be **–2,896.41** (the interest paid over the last 24 months).
3. Hit X↔Y.
4. The value should be **–1,118.55** (principal reduction over the last 24 months).
5. Hit RCL, hit PV.
6. The value should be **17,505.01** (the remaining balance after the last 24 months, which is the remaining balance after 5 years on the original amount).

To make yourself a believer, do the following:

Calculator Steps

1. *Clear registers.*
2. Enter 20,000, hit PV.
3. Enter 167.29, hit CHS, hit PMT.
4. Enter 8, hit blue g key, hit i.
5. Enter 60, hit yellow f key, hit n.
6. The value should be **–7,542.41** (total interest paid over the last 60 months).
7. Hit X↔Y.
8. The value should be **–2,494.99** (total principal reduction over the last 60 months).

9. Hit RCL, then PV.

10. The value should be **17,505.01** (the new balance after making the last 60 payments).

Example 3

Cy is offered a $35,000 mortgage (payment originally based on 10 years at 10%) that will pay $462.53 per month for the remaining 10 years. How much should he pay if he desires a 15% return on his investment?

Calculator Steps

1. Enter 15, hit blue g key, hit i.
2. Enter 10, hit blue g key, hit n.
3. Enter 462.53, hit CHS, hit PMT.
4. Hit PV.
5. This should give the value **28,668.93**.
6. *Do not clear calculator.*

Most purchasers of mortgages prefer a return of 20%. Since the information is still in your calculator, do not clear. Do the following:

Calculator Steps

1. Enter 20, hit blue g key, hit i.
2. Hit PV.
3. This should give a value of **23,933.58**.

An investor desiring a 20% return is willing to pay $23,933,58 for a $35,000 mortgage. Why would a bank be willing to sell a mortgage at a discount like this? Banks like to free up long-term money in order to make short-term loans, which command a higher interest rate.

Example 4

Dick is offered a building with lease payments of $12,000 a year for 20 years with no increase in rental payment. What should he pay for the building if an 11% return is desired?

Calculator Steps

1. Enter 11, hit i (since payments are annual, we do not hit the blue g key).
2. Enter 20, hit n (remember, annually).
3. Enter 12,000, hit CHS, hit PMT.
4. Hit PV.
5. The value should be **95,559.94**.

Example 5

How much should Sharon pay for a piece of land that can be sold in 5 years for $180,000 if a 14.5% return is desired?

Calculator Steps

1. Enter 14.5, hit i.
2. Enter 5, hit n.
3. Enter 180,000, hit FV.
4. Hit PV.
5. Value on the screen should be **–91,462.92** (again, the HP-12C represents payouts as a negative).

Example 6

If Sharon (in Problem 5) is able to buy the piece of land for $100,000, how much would she have to sell it for to yield a 20% return?

1. Enter 100,000, hit CHS, hit PV.
2. Enter 5, hit n.
3. Enter 20, hit i.
4. Hit FV.
5. The value on the screen should be **248,832**.

Example 7

Take $5,000 and compound it quarterly at 9% for 5 years.

1. Enter 5,000, hit CHS, hit PV.
2. Enter 2.25, hit i. (Interest rate must be given per period. Since there are 4 quarterly periods in one year, you must divide 9 by 4.)
3. Enter 20, hit n (4 periods per year for 20 years).
4. Hit FV.
5. The value should be **7,802.55**.

This example is designed to show how important it is to enter the correct information regarding the interest rate per period and the number of periods.

Example 8

Given a $90,000 mortgage at 10.5% for 30 years:
Find the monthly payment

1. Enter 90,000, hit PV.
2. Enter 10.5, hit blue g key, hit i.
3. Enter 30, hit blue g key, hit n.
4. Hit PMT
5. The monthly payment is **$823.27**.

Find the amount of interest saved and the number of years the mortgage term would be shortened if the borrower paid an additional $100 on each monthly payment.

1. Enter 90,000, hit PV.
2. Enter 10.5, hit blue g key, hit i.
3. Enter 923.27, hit CHS, hit PMT.
4. Hit n.
5. The value should be **221** (the number of months required to pay off the loan of $90,000).
6. Enter 221, hit ENTER, enter 12, hit the divide key.
7. The value should be **18.42** (the number of years to pay off the loan).
8. Enter 360, hit ENTER, hit 823.26, hit times key.
9. The value should be **296,373.60**.
10. Hit ENTER, enter 90,000, hit the subtraction key.

11. The value should be **206,373.60** (the amount of interest due in the original loan).
12. Hit STO, hit key 1.
13. Enter 923.27, hit ENTER, hit 221, hit the times key.
14. The value should be **204,042.67**.
15. Hit ENTER, enter 90,000, hit the subtraction key.
16. The value should be **114,042.67**.
17. Hit STO, hit key 2.
18. Hit RCL, hit key 1, hit ENTER, hit RCL, hit key 2, hit the subtraction key.
19. The value should be **$92,330.93**.
20. Clear the calculator.

> **Note:** This problem illustrates that, by paying an additional $100 per month, the borrower can reduce the mortgage term by approximately 12 years and save over $90,000 in interest payments!

Money today will not be worth the same amount a year from now. This concept is commonly called the *time value* of money. To compensate for this, we can discount any future money back to today's value by using the idea of *present value* versus *future value*.

Example 9

We are to receive $20,000 from an investment property one year from today. To find out what this money would be worth in today's value, let us discount this at a rate of 12%. (The discount rate is an arbitrary number but usually reflects the rate of return you would like to receive on any investment.)

Calculator Steps

1. Enter 20,000, hit FV.
2. Enter 1, hit n.
3. Enter 12, hit i.
4. Hit PV.
5. The value should be **–17,857.14**.

Now suppose you have the following stream of after-tax cash flows over the next six years and in the sixth year you sell the property for a net profit of $29,000.

Year	Cash Flows	Net Profit from Sale	Discounted Value
1	$20,000		$17,857
2	$20,400		$16,263
3	$30,000		$21,353
4	$20,600		$13,092
5	$20,200		$11,462
6	$10,800	$29,000	$20,164
By totaling the discounted values, we get $100,191.			

If this number is the same as the amount invested originally, then the true internal rate of return for this investor is exactly 12%. Rarely does this happen. Therefore, the idea of net present value is used. If the original investment is *higher* than this number, then the return is *less* than 12%. If the original investment is *lower* than this number, then the return is *higher* than 12%.

Our goal in later chapters will be to find the exact internal rate of return.

PROBLEM SET 3

1. William Andrew is considering the purchase of a parcel of vacant land that is expected to have a value of $500,000 five years from now. The investor's required rate of return is 15% per year. How much should the investor pay for the land?

2. An apartment building has a current market value of $75,000. If the value of the property is expected to increase by 5% per year, what will the property be worth in 3 years?

3. You promise to pay a lender $631.93 per month for 25 years. The lender wants to earn 12% per year. How much will the lender loan you today?

4. Using the facts in Problem 3, how much will you owe at the end of:

    a. 5 years?

    b. 10 years?

5. A real estate investment was purchased for $1,000,000 and was sold 6years later for $1,340,000. What was the average percentage increase in the property's value per year?

6. A mortgage loan of $1,000,000 was made at an interest rate of 12.5% for 20 years.

    a. What would the *monthly* payment be?

    b. What would the *annual* payment be? (*Hint:* It is *not* 12 times the answer to a.)

    c. Allocate the payments for years 1 through 5 between interest and principal for part b.

    d. What is the amount outstanding at the end of 8 years?

7. A mortgage loan of $450,000 was made with payments of $5,417 per month for 25 years. What is the interest rate on the loan?

8. Calculate the monthly mortgage payment and find the total interest paid for $100,000 at 11% for:

    a. 30 years

    b. 20 years

    c. 15 years

9. Calculate the monthly payment and find the total interest paid on $100,000 for 20 years at:
   a. 8.5%
   b. 9.5%
   c. 11.5%

10. Given $100,000 at 11.5% for 30 years, find the *new loan term* and *interest saved* if the following additional principal payments are made per month:
    a. $50
    b. $100
    c. $200

11. If $5,000 is placed in a savings account earning 11.5% interest, how much will be in the account in:
    a. 5 years?
    b. 10 years?
    c. 25 years?

12. A savings plan provides for $100 per month to be set aside. It will earn 8.5% interest. How much will be in the account in:
    a. 5 years?
    b. 10 years?
    c. 25 years?

13. An investor has 10 ranges in an apartment house. The ranges must be replaced in 5 years at a cost of $500 each. How much must be set aside each year if the amounts set aside earn:
    a. 8% per year?
    b. 10% per year?

14. How much could Jessica, wishing to earn 15% per year, invest in land if the land is expected to be worth $300,000 in:
    a. 5 years?
    b. 10 years?
    c. 25 years?

15. Betty wishes to earn 10%. How much could Betty pay for land today if the land is expected to be worth $300,000 in:
    a. 5 years?
    b. 10 years?
    c. 25 years?

16. A mortgage pays back $6,000 per year for 20 years. How much could Lou pay today for the mortgage to get a return of:
    a. 8%?
    b. 10%?
    c. 20%?

17. A mortgage pays back $6,000 per year for 20 years. In addition to the 20 regular $6,000 payments, the mortgage also has a balloon payment due the 20th year of $80,000. How much could Ross (an investor) pay today for the mortgage to get a return of:

    a. 8%?

    b. 10%?

    c. 20%?

18. What is the monthly mortgage payment on a 10.5% mortgage for $80,000 for:

    a. 10 years?

    b. 20 years?

    c. 30 years?

19. What will the remaining mortgage balance be after 5 years on each of the mortgages in Problem 18?

    a. _____

    b. _____

    c. _____

20. How much interest is earned if $5,500 is invested today at 10% annual interest, compounded monthly, if the initial sum is allowed to accrue interest for 3 years?

21. How much interest is earned under the circumstances in Problem 20, except that annual compounding is used? (Note the effect of more frequent compounding.)

22. If $2,000 is invested each year for a total of 40 years at a 15% annual compound rate, how much money will accumulate?

23. You wish to be assured of having $20,000 ten years from now to send your child to college. How much must you invest *each year* if you could be guaranteed of earning 9% compounded annually on your funds placed on deposit?

24. You own a property that was projected to require a new roof at the end of 5 years from today, costing an estimated $5,500. If you can reinvest your capital at 8% annual interest compounded monthly, how much must you set aside from earnings each month to be assured of having the necessary capital?

25. How much would you be willing to pay for an investment that has an estimated market value of $51,000 seven years from today if you wish to earn 12% on the investment?

26. What is the present worth of $1,000,000 to be received at the end of 25 years, discounted at 15%?

27. What should Jug (an investor) be willing to pay for an investment that promises the following stream of future cash payments, if the discount rate is 10.5%?

n	$
1	3,000
2	4,000
3	5,000
4	6,000
5	7,000

28. What is the present value of the following income stream when discounted at 10.5%?

n	$
1	0
2	0
3	0
4	3,000
5	4,000
6	5,000
7	6,000
8	7,000

29. If you wish to borrow $7,500 for 15 years at 9%, what *annual* payments are required to pay off the loan?

30. What is the remaining balance on a 20-year, 10.25%, $50,000 mortgage with annual payments:

  a. after the 4th payment has been made?

  b. after the 12th payment has been made?

31. An investor has the following cash flows:

Year	Cash Flow
0	−$100,000
1	$ 15,000
2	$ 20,000
3	$ 18,000
4	$ 12,000
5	$ 85,000

If the investor's required rate of return is 15%, what is the net present value?

32. Using the facts in Problem 31, compute the internal rate of return.

33. What is the present value of the following?

Year	Cash Flow	At 10%	At 30%
1	$25	_____	_____
2	$32	_____	_____
3	$28	_____	_____
4	$11	_____	_____

34. Land is purchased for $60,000, paying $10,000 cash down and the balance due in 5 years. Interest only is to be paid during the 5 years at 8% with a balloon in 5 years. The land is rented for $5,000 a year, and real estate taxes run $1,000 a year. It is estimated that the land could be sold at the end of 5 years for $100,000. Complete the following statements:

   a. The purchaser's initial investment is $ _____.

   b. The cash flow per year during ownership but before the sale of the property is $ _____.

   c. If selling costs are estimated at $5,000, the net sales proceeds at the time of sale before tax on sale are $ _____.

   d. If the tax on the sale is $5,000, the net sales proceeds after tax are $ _____.

   e. The present value of the future income from the land purchase, discounted at 10%, is $ _____.

   f. The internal rate of return is _____%.

Chapter 4

COLLECTING AND ANALYZING DATA

Outline
  I. Collection of Annual Property Data
  II. Calculating Annual After-Tax Cash Flows
  III. Calculating Returns and Net Proceeds from a Sale

This chapter is devoted solely to the organizing and analyzing of the data in Example 1. It is extremely helpful to have the example problem and the answer sheets beside you as you read the chapter. (I suggest that you make a copy of each page.)

The information in the example is fundamental to most properties. The assessed value can be found by contacting the county assessment office. Note that the assessment is usually broken down into land and improvement. This is important for calculating the depreciation on the improvement. In this example, the land value is considered to be 10% of the total assessed value.

Example 1: Four-Unit Apartment

Property price	$100,000
Down payment	20%
Interest rate	11%
Term	20 years
Payments	Monthly
Land value	$10,000
Two one-bedroom apts.	$330 per month each
Two two-bedroom apts.	$360 per month each
Legal expenses	$70
License	$25
Property insurance	$170
School tax	$850
County tax	$550
Trash	$175
Snow removal	$100
Electric	$300
Oil	$1,954
Water and sewer	$600

Straight-line depreciation over 27.5 years	
Tax bracket of buyer	28%
Inflation rate	3.5% per year
Assessed value	$ 23,900
Costs to sell property	$ 7,500

Problem:

- Fill out an Annual Property Operating Data (APOD) form, and then complete a Cash Flow Analysis form (CFA) for 5 years.
- Then calculate the net proceeds after the sale of the property.

The following is a line-by-line explanation of the *Annual Property Operating Data* form, commonly called an APOD:

1. *Scheduled rental income:* This reflects the amount of annual income that should be received according to the written and signed leases (When purchasing an investment property, you should review and verify the terms of all leases.) In this case, the $16,560 is found by:

   2 (apts.) × $330 = $660 for 12 months = $7,920 and

   2 (apts.) × $360 = $720 for 12 months = $8,640 then

   $7,920 + $8,640 = $16,560

2. *Vacancy and credit losses:* This may be difficult to evaluate for smaller properties. When a tenant moves out, it usually means the loss of rent for one month. This is the necessary time to renovate the apartment and screen new tenants. In larger complexes that have been in operation for several years, a pattern of vacancy may be established that enables a percentage to be associated with vacancy and credit loss.

3. *Effective rental income:* This is found by subtracting the Vacancy and credit losses (2) from Scheduled rental income (1).

4. *Other income:* It has become more common to have other income in multifamily properties. This is due primarily to the use of pay washers and dryers on the premises for the tenants.

5. *Gross operating income:* This is found by adding the Effective rental income (3) and Other income (4). Lines 7–29 represent the operating expenses on an annual basis for the property. All expenses should be verified and documented if possible. Most of the expenses are self-explanatory but some comments are necessary.

7. *Accounting:* You may not find it necessary to retain an accountant. With the many changes in tax laws, however, having a qualified accountant review any tax consequences becomes important (while owning the property or prior to purchase).

8. *Advertising:* Any time you have a vacancy, you need advertising, primarily in the local newspaper. With larger properties, it may become necessary to establish a contract with the newspaper to get a discount on the advertising.

9. *Property insurance:* Both fire and liability are musts.

ANNUAL PROPERTY OPERATING DATA

Name: Mr. Jack the Investor

Property Address: 1234 Anywhere Dr.

Type of Property: 4-unit apartment

		Date:		
		Price:	$100,000.00	
		Equity:	$ 20,000.00	
		Loans:	$ 80,000.00	

Assessed/Appraised Values

			Mortgage:	1st	2nd
Land:	$2,390	10.00%	Balance:	$ 80,000.00	$0.00
Improvement:	$21,510	90.00%	Int. Rate:	11.00%	10.50%
Personal Prop.:		0.00%	Term:	20	20
Total:	$23,900	100.00%	Payment:	$825.75	$0.00

	1	2	3	Comments
1	SCHEDULED RENTAL INCOME		$16,560	
2	Less: Vacancy and Credit Losses		$0	
3	EFFECTIVE RENTAL INCOME		$16,560	
4	Plus: Other Income			
5	GROSS OPERATING INCOME		$16,560	
6	OPERATING EXPENSES			
7	Accounting	$0		
8	Advertising	$0		
9	Property Insurance	$170		
10	Property Management	$0		
11	Personal Property Taxes	$0		
12	School Taxes	$850		
13	Municipal & County Taxes	$550		
14	Repairs and Maintenance	$0		
15	Laundry	$0		
16	Lawn Care	$0		
17	Snow Removal	$100		
18	Legal	$70		
19	Licenses/Permits	$25		
20	Cable TV	$0		
21	Trash	$175		
22	Supplies	$0		
23	Electricity	$300		
24	Gas	$0		
25	Oil	$1,954		
26	Water and sewer	$600		
27	Telephone	$0		
28	Miscellaneous	$0		
29				
	less			
30	TOTAL OPERATING EXPENSES		$4,794	
	equals			
31	NET OPERATING INCOME		$11,766	
	less			
32	ANNUAL DEBT SERVICE		$9,909	
	equals			
33	BEFORE-TAX CASH FLOW		$1,857	

10. *Property management:* Whether you do the managing or you hire some-one, you must deal with this expense.

11–13. *Personal property taxes, School taxes, and County and municipal taxes:* These must be paid, whether you like it or not!

14–17. *Repairs and maintenance, Laundry, Lawn care, Snow removal:* These are self-explanatory.

18. *Legal:* An attorney becomes vital when there are concerns about inter-preting leases and landlord-tenant relationships. If a tenant must be evicted, *use an expert.*

19. *License/permits:* Many communities require licenses if a property ex-ceeds two units. Check with the local zoning authorities to be sure. Even if a property is being used as an apartment house, it may not be a legal use.

20–27. *Cable TV, Trash, Supplies, Electricity, Gas, Oil, Water and sewer, Telephone:* These are self-explanatory.

28. *Miscellaneous:* Include any expenses here that do not fit into the other categories.

29. *Other:* Include any expenses here that do not fit into the other categories.

30. *Total operating expenses:* This is found by adding the input in rows 7 through 29.

31. *Net operating income:* To find this, subtract *Total operating expenses (30)* from *Gross Operating Income (5).*

32. *Annual debt service:* Find this by multiplying the *Monthly mortgage pay-ment* ($825.75) by 12, which equals $9,909 (rounded to the nearest dollar).

33. *Before-tax cash flow:* This is found by subtracting *Annual debt service (32)* from *Net operating income (31).*

If you follow the steps on this form, line 33 shows how much money should be in your pocket at the end of one year of owning this property. A decision about whether to buy or sell could be made at this point, but it is much wiser to make a decision after finding out how much will be in your pocket *after taxes.*

The following is a line-by-line explanation of the *Cash Flow Analysis* form, commonly called a CFA:

1. *1st mortgage:* This shows the amount borrowed, the term, the interest rate, the monthly payment, and the annual debt service.

2. *2nd mortgage:* This shows the amount borrowed, the term, the interest rate, the monthly payment, and the annual debt service.

3. *1st mortgage bal. (EOY):* This is the remaining balance of the first mort-gage at the end of one year of payments.

4. *2nd mortgage bal. (EOY):* This is the remaining balance of the second mortgage at the end of one year of payments.

5. *Remaining balance (EOY):* The remaining balance is the total of lines (3) and (4).

CASH FLOW ANALYSIS

Name:_____   Date: _____

MORTGAGE DATA

Encumbrances		Beginning Balance	Remaining Term	Interest Rate	Monthly Payment	Annual Debt
1	1st Mortgage	$80,000	20	11.00%	$825.75	$9,909
2	2nd Mortgage	$0	20	10.50%	$0.00	$0

		year 1	year 2	year 3	year 4	year 5
3	1st Mortgage Bal. (EOY)	$78,833	$77,532	$76,079	$74,459	$72,651
4	2nd Mortgage Bal. (EOY)	$0	$0	$0	$0	$0
5	Remaining Balance (EOY)	$78,833	$77,532	$76,079	$74,459	$72,651
6	Principal Paid (EOY)	$1,167	$1,302	$1,452	$1,620	$1,808
7	Total Interest (EOY)	$8,742	$8,607	$8,457	$8,289	$8,101

TAXABLE INCOME

8	Gross Operating Income	$16,560	$17,140	$17,739	$18,360	$19,003
	less					
9	Total Operating Expense	$4,794	$4,962	$5,135	$5,315	$5,501
	equals					
10	Net Operating Income	$11,766	$12,178	$12,604	$13,045	$13,502
	less					
11	Total Interest	$8,742	$8,607	$8,457	$8,289	$8,101
	less					
12	Depreciation	$3,273	$3,273	$3,273	$3,273	$3,273
	equals					
13	TAXABLE INCOME	($249)	$298	$874	$1,483	$2,128

CASH FLOW AFTER TAXES

14	Net Operating Income	$11,766	$12,178	$12,604	$13,045	$13,502
	less					
15	Annual Debt Service	$9,909	$9,909	$9,909	$9,909	$9,909
	less					
16	Capital Additions	$0	$0	$0	$0	$0
	equals					
17	Cash Flow before Taxes	$1,857	$2,269	$2,695	$3,136	$3,593
	less					
18	Tax Liability	($70)	$83	$245	$415	$596
	equals					
19	CASH FLOW AFTER TAXES	$1,927	$2,186	$2,450	$2,721	$2,997

Inflation rate   3.50%
Tax rate   28.00%

Note: For years 2–5, the Gross operating income and the Total operating expenses were increased on a projected basis using the inflation rate given as 3.5% per year. The calculations are:

	Year 2	Year 3	Year 4	Year 5
8.	(1.035) (16,560)	(1.035) (17,140)	(1.035) (17,739)	(1.035) (18,360)
9.	(1.035) (4,794)	(1.035) (4,962)	(1.035) (5,135)	(1.035) (5,315)

---

6. *Principal paid (EOY):* The total amount of principal paid on all mortgages appears on this line. Remember, as you pay off your mortgage it is as if you are putting more money down on the property.

7. *Total interest (EOY):* Important as a write-off for taxes, this is the total amount of interest paid for all mortgages.

8. *Gross operating income:* Year one should be the same as line 5 on the APOD form. (See the note regarding years 2–5.)

9. *Total operating expenses:* Year one should be the same as line 30 on the APOD form. (See the note regarding years 2–5.)

10. *Net operating income:* To find this, subtract Total operating expenses (9) from Gross operating income (8).

11. *Total interest:* This should be the same as line 7 above.

12. *Depreciation:* Divide the improvement value by the useful life of the property. In this case, the improvement value is 90% of the total value (.90 × $100,000), which equals $90,000, divided by a useful life of 27.5 years, which gives straight-line depreciation each year of $3,273.

    The formula for straight-line depreciation is:

    $$\frac{\text{Improvement value}}{\text{Useful life}} = \frac{\$90,000}{27.5} = \$3,273$$

13. *Taxable income:* Subtract Total interest (11) and Depreciation (12) from Net operating income (10). You might get negative answers, even though this property has a positive before-tax cash flow. The IRS views this property as having a negative flow in the first year.

14. *Net operating income:* This is the same as line 10.

15. *Annual debt service:* Take this from line 32 on the APOD form.

16. *Capital additions:* These include any large expenditures, such as a new roof, heat plant, etc.

17. *Cash flow before taxes:* Subtract Annual debt service (15) and Capital additions (16) from Net operating income (14).

18. *Tax liability:* Multiply Taxable income (13) times the investor's tax bracket (in this case, 28%) found on the information sheet: $249 × .28 = $70.

19. *Cash flow after taxes:* Subtract Tax liability (18) from Cash flow before taxes (17).

Remember: In basic math, when subtracting a negative, you actually do addition.

Example:
$1,857 – (–70) is actually $1,857 + 70 = $1,927

The following is a line-by-line explanation of the *Net Sales Proceeds:*

1. *Original basis:* This is the purchase price of the property.
2. *Capital improvements:* Total of the major improvements to the property, such as a new roof, heat plant, etc.
3. *Selling expenses:* This refers to the costs to sell the property, including real estate commission, advertising, etc.
4. *Depreciation:* Include the total depreciation accumulated while owning the property.
5. *Partial sales:* This refers to any part of the property that may have been sold during ownership.
6. *Adjusted cost basis:* Add Capital improvements (2) and Selling expenses (3) to the Original basis (1), and then subtract Depreciation (4) and Partial sales (5).
7. *Sale price:* This is the price the property is going to sell for today or on a projected basis, using a given inflation criterion.
8. *Adjusted cost basis:* This is the same as line 6.
9. *Capital gain:* Subtract Adjusted cost basis (8) from Sale price (7).
10. *Capital gain:* This is the same as line 9.
11. *Tax bracket:* Use the tax bracket of the investor, in this example given as 28%.
12. *Total tax:* Multiply Capital gain (10) by Tax bracket (11).
13. *Sale price:* This is the same as line 7.
14. *Selling expenses:* This is the same as line 3.
15. *Mortgage balances:* Get this amount from the Cash Flow Analysis under year 5, row 5.
16. *Tax on gain:* This is the same as line 12.
17. *Net sales proceeds:* Subtract Selling expenses (14) and Mortgage balances (15) and Tax on gain (16) from Sale price (13).

NET SALES PROCEEDS

Calculating Adjusted Cost Basis

1.	Original basis	$100,000
2.	Plus capital improvements	
3.	Plus selling expenses	$7,500
4.	Minus depreciation	$16,365
5.	Minus partial sales	
	Equals	
6.	Adjusted cost basis	$91,135

Calculating the Gain upon Sale

7.	Sales price	$118,769
8.	Minus adjusted cost basis	$91,135
	Equals	
9.	Capital gain	$27,634

Calculating the Tax on the Gain

10.	Capital gain	$27,634
11.	Times tax bracket	28.00%
	Equals	
12.	Total tax	$7,738

Calculating the Net Sales Proceeds

13.	Sales price	$118,769
14.	Minus selling expenses	$7,500
15.	Minus mortgage balances	$72,651
16.	Minus tax on gain	$7,738
	Equals	
17.	Net sales proceeds	$30,880

PROBLEM SET 4

1.

Sale price	$164,000
Down payment	$ 24,000
1st mortgage	$ 90,000 at 12% for 20 years
2nd mortgage	$ 50,000 at 10.5% for 20 years (5 year balloon)

Four 2-bedroom apartments: two at $350 per apartment per month and two at $400 per apartment per month

Two 1-bedroom apartments at $300 per apartment per month

Expenses:

School taxes	$1,250
Municipal and county taxes	$ 350
Insurance	$ 400
Electricity	$ 200
Water & sewer	$ 600
Trash	$ 225
Heat	$2,000
Advertising	$ 50
Licenses	$ 30
Maintenance	$ 200
Snow removal	$ 100
Vacancy rate	5%
Buyer's tax bracket	38.5%
Straight-line depreciation with a 27.5-year useful life	
Land value	9% of the total price
Inflation rate for rent and expenses (and appreciation)	3.5%
Costs to sell the property after 5 years	8% of the sale price

    a. Analyze the property using APOD and CFA for 5 years.

    b. Complete a Net Sales Proceeds sheet.

2. Compare the following properties:

	Apt. A	**Apt. B**
List price	$50,000	$80,000
Down payment	$10,000	$20,000
9% interest/annual payment of	$ 4,000	$ 9,000
Land	$10,000	$10,000
Remaining life	27.5 yrs.	27.5 yrs.
Gross income	$ 7,000	$11,000
Operating expense	$ 2,000	$ 3,000
Inflation and appreciation rate	5%	6%
Tax bracket	30%	30%

   a. Do an APOD and CFA for 3 years.

   b. Decide which of the two properties has a better return.

3.

	4-unit	6-unit	8-Unit
List price	$140,000	$152,000	$160,000
Down payment	$ 20,000	$ 25,000	$ 25,000
Financing			
Amount	$120,000	$127,000	$135,000
Interest rate	11.5%	11%	9.5%
Term	20 yrs.	20 yrs.	25 yrs.
Payment (P&I)	$ 15,565/yr.	$ 15,948/yr.	$ 15,200/yr. (This is not a mistake.)
Depreciation Information			
Land	$ 42,000	$ 30,400	$ 40,000
Improvements (27.5-year life)	$ 84,000	$106,400	$100,000
Personal Property (7-year life)	$ 14,000	$ 15,200	$ 20,000
Method	St. Line	St. Line	St. line
Annual income	$ 21,000	$ 25,100	$ 24,100
Vacancy	$ 1,050	$ 1,757	$ 1,205
Estimated expenses	$ 6,500	$ 6,800	$ 6,895
Appreciation	5%/yr.	3.5%/yr.	4.5%/yr.
Tax bracket	28%	28%	28%

   a. Complete an APOD and CFA for 3 years.

   b. Rank each investment on the basis of:
   Cash flow
   Total return in dollars
   Total return to equity

4. Elizabeth was considering different methods of acquiring the 8-unit property in Problem 3. She had shown the property to her father. He was interested in going in with her on the purchase of the building, but he was not willing to go into debt.

   Alternative 1: He proposed that Elizabeth put up $25,000 cash, and he would put up $135,000 in cash from the sale of his home. He would then move into one of the apartments, and they could operate as partners.

   Alternative 2: Elizabeth could borrow $50,000 from her father and put up $25,000 of her own for a down payment of $75,000. From talking with the owner, Elizabeth learned that there was an existing $85,000 mortgage at 9.5% with annual payments of $9,400 that could be assumed. Elizabeth's father would charge 9% over 20 years with no balloon.

   Alternative 3: The seller could carry back a $50,000 second contract at 10% with payments of $5,800 per year (and a balloon at the end of 14 years). Elizabeth and her father would then borrow $100,000 at 10.5% for 20 years and only put $10,000 down.

   Determine which of the three alternatives would be best for Elizabeth, or offer a better one!

Chapter 5

DISCOUNTED CASH FLOW METHODS

Outline
I. Internal Rate of Return
   a. Regular method
   b. Reinvestment method
II. Financial Manager's Rate of Return
   a. Safe rate method
   b. Borrowing rate method

I. Internal Rate of Return

Internal rate of return is a trial and error method. The investor attempts to determine the percentage rate of return necessary to make the anticipated inflows equal to the initial investment outlay. The interest rate that equates the present value of the expected future receipts with the cost of the investment outlay is called the *internal rate of return*.

In the present value method, you *discount* the future annual cash flows (find the present value of the future cash), and the net sales proceeds at the end of the estimated holding period, by the rate of return desired by the investor. The dollar amount found is then compared with the initial investment. If the present value is equal to the initial outlay, then the discount percentage used is the internal rate of return.

Method 1 for Internal Rate of Return: The Regular Method

			Discount at 15%	Discount at 25%
Year 0	Initial investment	$10,000		
Year 1	Annual Total Cash Flow	$ 2,000	$ 1,739.13	$1,600.00
Year 2	ATCF	$ 2,000	$ 1,512.29	$1,280.00
Year 3	ATCF	$ 2,000	$ 1,315.03	$1,024.00
Year 4	ATCF	$ 2,000	$ 1,143.51	$ 819.20
Year 5	ATCF and net sales proceeds	$13,000	$ 6,463.30	$4,259.84
			$12,173.26	$8,983.04

Compare the total from each column to the initial outlay and discuss IRR. Then calculate IRR on your HP-12C:

1. Enter 10,000, hit CHS, hit blue g key, hit PV(CFo).
2. Enter 2,000, hit blue g key, hit PMT(CFj).
3. Enter 2,000, hit blue g key, hit PMT(CFj).
4. Enter 2,000, hit blue g key, hit PMT(CFj).
5. Enter 2,000, hit blue g key, hit PMT(CFj).
6. Enter 13,000, hit blue g key, hit PMT(CFj).
7. Hit yellow f key, hit FV(IRR).
8. The value should be **21.3097%**.

Now verify that what you have done is correct. Go back and discount each cash amount at the IRR number, and your total should be equal to your initial investment.

Use	21.3097%
2,000	$1,648.67
2,000	$1,359.06
2,000	$1,120.32
2,000	$ 923.52
13,000	$4,948.41
	$9,999.98

Discounted cash flow methods have two weaknesses:

1. They assume that the future cash inflows can be reinvested at the same rate as the internal rate of return.
2. They do not handle negative cash flows accurately.

Find the net present value of each of the following cash flows:

Year:	Cash Flow	Present Value (10%)	Present Value (20%)	Present Value (30%)
1	$3,600.00	$3,272.72	$3,000.00	$2,769.23
2	($4,310.00)	($3,561.98)	($2,993.06)	($2,550.30)
3	$1,716.00	$1,289.26	$ 993.06	$ 781.07

The sum of each column is *$1,000.00*. What is the internal rate of return? That question leads us to the second method.

Method 2 for Internal Rate of Return: Reinvestment Method

The cash flows are adjusted by the reinvestment rate at which funds received can reasonably be invested. In the following chart, this rate is 8%.

Year	Cash Flow		5th-year Value
0	($10,000)	(Represents initial investment)	
1	$ 2,000	(Reinvested at 8% for 4 years)	$ 2,721
2	$ 2,000	(Reinvested at 8% for 3 years)	$ 2,519
3	$ 2,000	(Reinvested at 8% for 2 years)	$ 2,333
4	$ 2,000	(Reinvested at 8% for 1 year)	$ 2,160
5	$ 2,000	(Property is sold and net proceeds = $11,000)	$13,000

This treats each cash flow as if it were earning interest at 8% instead of assuming that it earns interest at the IRR rate.

On your calculator, you treat your $10,000 as an initial outlay. The total of the last column represents your cash return over the 5 years.

Calculator Steps

1. Enter $10,000, hit CHS, hit PV.
2. Enter $22,733, hit FV.
3. Enter 5, hit n.
4. Hit i.
5. The value should be **17.85%**.

This number represents the internal rate of return.

II. Financial Manager's Rate of Return (FMRR)

Method 1 for Financial Manager's Rate of Return: Safe Rate Method

For handling negative cash flows, one alternative is to set aside money today for future negative cash flows. Each negative cash flow is adjusted at the safe rate as follows:

1. If no positive cash flows precede the negative cash flow, the negative cash flows are discounted to the present at the safe rate and are considered additional initial investments.
2. If positive flows precede negative cash flows, assume that the positive cash flow can be used to pay the negative cash flows that follow it, that is, until the positive cash flow plus any safe rate of interest it may earn is exhausted. The following example shows a purchase of land for $20,000 with negative cash flows each year until the property is sold for net proceeds of $90,000.

Year	Cash Flow	Discounted at 8% and Considered as Part of the Initial Investment
0	($20,000)	
1	($10,500)	$9,722 (discounted at 8% for 1 year)
2	($10,500)	$9,002 (discounted at 8% for 2 years)
3	($10,500)	$8,335 (discounted at 8% for 3 years)
4	($10,500)	$7,718 (discounted at 8% for 4 years)

Therefore the investor actually sets aside $54,777 as the initial investment.

Calculator Steps to Find FMRR

1. Enter 54,777, hit CHS, hit PV.
2. Enter 90,000, hit FV.
3. Enter 4, hit n.
4. Hit i.
5. The value should be **13.22%**.

Now look at an example in which a positive cash flow precedes negative flows.

Example

Given the following information:

Initial investment	$10,000
1st year cash flow (positive) that can be reinvested at a safe rate of 5%	$4,000
2nd year flow (negative)	$2,000
3rd year flow (negative)	$3,000
4th year flow (negative)	$4,000
The property is sold at beginning of 5th year with net proceeds of $30,000.	

The chart on the following page shows how the positive flow plus any earned interest is used to offset future negative cash flows. Once the positive flow no longer covers the negative flow, the investor must consider setting aside money at a safe rate to cover the future negative flows.

Initial investment is the sum of $10,000 + $596 + $3,291 = $13,887

Calculator Steps to Find FMRR

1. Enter 13,887, hit CHS, hit PV.
2. Enter $30,000, hit FV.
3. Enter 5, hit n.
4. Hit i.
5. The value should be **16.65%**.

Year	Cash Flow	
0	($10,000)	Initial investment
1	$ 4,000	Earns 5% interest for one year ($4,200).
2	($ 2,000)	Use the money in the bank to pay for loss: $4,200 – $2,000 leaves $2,200 to earn interest at 5%.
3	($ 3,000)	Now we have $2,310 in the bank but a loss of $3,000 causes a net loss of $690. Therefore, the investor must set aside an additional amount as an initial investment to cover the $690. You must discount $690 at 5% for 3 years. $596 becomes part of the initial investment.
4	($ 4,000)	This money must be covered by the initial investment; so discount it at 5% for 4 years ($3,291).
5	$30,000	The property is sold! This represents the net proceeds.

Method 2 for Financial Manager's Rate of Return— Borrowing Rate Method

Under this method, the investor chooses not to set aside enough cash in addition to the initial investment to cover the negative cash flows. The investor waits until the negative flows occur, borrows the funds to meet the negative cash flows, and then pays back the loan out of future cash inflows. Look at the previous problem, but this time borrow money at 12% every time there is a negative flow. Then pay your loans back upon the sale of the property. Notice these negative future values affect your expected net proceeds.

Year	Cash Flow	
0	$10,000	Initial investment
1	$ 4,000	Invested at 5% for 4 years: $4,862
2	($ 2,000)	Borrowed at 12% for 3 years: ($2,810)
3	($ 3,000)	Borrowed at 12% for 2 years: ($3,763)
4	($ 4,000)	Borrowed at 12% for 1 year: ($4,480)
5	$30,000	Net proceeds from the sale

After paying off the loan, the investor has left in the bank: $34,862 – $11,053 = $23,809

Calculator Steps to Find FMRR

1. Enter $10,000, hit CHS, hit PV.
2. Enter $23,809, hit FV.
3. Enter 5, hit n.
4. Hit i.
5. The value should be **18.95%**.

Comparing this with the preceding example makes it obvious that you can increase your own return by using someone else's money.

- *The IRR-regular method* discounts all cash flows, both positive and negative, at the same rate.
- *The IRR-reinvestment rate method* first adjusts cash flows by the rate that cash received can be reasonably invested.
- *The FMRR-safe rate method* is similar to the reinvestment rate method, but a safe rate is used to adjust cash flows so that the investor can be assured of meeting future cash obligations—and it is used only when negative cash flows are anticipated.
- *The FMRR-borrowing rate method* is used only when negative cash flows are anticipated and the negative flows are adjusted by a loan rate, with the investor hoping to repay the loan with future cash flows.

PROBLEM SET 5

1. Consider the following set of cash flows and reversion:

Year	ATCF	Net Proceeds
0	($80,000)	
1	$10,000	
2	$20,000	
3	$20,000	
4	$25,000	$50,000

  a. What is the net present value if discounting at 10%?
  b. What is the net present value if discounting at 20%?
  c. Calculate the actual internal rate of return.
  d. Prove that the IRR is correct by using it to discount your cash flows.

2. David Russell is considering an investment with the following expected cash flows and sales proceeds:

Year	ATCF	Net Proceeds
1	$10,000	
2	$10,500	
3	$12,000	
4	$11,000	
5	$13,000	
6	$10,000	$140,000

What is the maximum the investor can pay if he desires a 15% rate of return?

3. Willie is considering an investment that has a total cost of $500,000. The following information is obtained from analyzing the market:

Average rent	$345 per unit per month
Number of units	28 rental units
Vacancy rate	7% of the gross annual rent
Operating expenses	$48,000
Loan-to-value ratio	.80
Interest rate on mortgage	10%
Term	25 years (with annual payments)
Depreciable basis	85% of purchase price
Depreciation method	Straight-line over 27.5 years
Expected appreciation	Total of 10% over the holding period
Holding period	5 years
Tax bracket of investor	30%
Inflation	Use 3% per year for increase of rental income and expenses.
Costs to sell property	$35,000
Required rate of return by investor	*16%*

   a. Find the internal rate of return.
   b. Decide if the investor should buy the property.

4. Land was purchased for $80,000, paying $10,000 down and the balance due in 5 years. *Interest only* was to be paid at 9% with a balloon in 5 years. The land was rented for $7,300 a year and real estate taxes were $1,000 a year. It was estimated that the land could be sold at the end of the 5 years for $120,000.

   a. The purchaser's initial investment was _____.
   b. The cash flow per year during ownership but before the sale of the property was _____.
   c. If selling costs were estimated at $8,400, the net sales proceeds before taxes were _____.
   d. If the tax on the sale was $8,000, the net sales proceeds after taxes were _____.
   e. The present value of the future income from the land purchase, discounted at 10%, is _____.
   f. The internal rate of return is _____.

5. Betty's property had cash flows as follows:

Initial cash outflow	$20,000
Cash inflow in 5 years	$40,000
(No other cash flow resulted.)	

   a. The present value of the future flow of income, discounted at 12%, is _____.

    b. The present value of the future flow of income, discounted at 20%, is _____.

    c. The internal rate of return on the investment is _____.

6. For a $240,000 mortgage to be amortized with annual payments over 20 years at 8.75% interest:

    a. What will the annual payments be?

    b. What is the remaining mortgage balance after five payments?

    c. How much interest has been paid up to and including the fifth payment?

7. Based on the following information, complete statements a through d:

Asking price	$115,000
Down payment	$20,000
Financing:	$95,000 carried on contract at 9% interest with payments of $9,500 per year
Gross operating income (after vacancies)	$15,000 per year
Expenses:	
Real estate taxes	$3,500
Insurance	$430
Utilities	$510
Interest on contract	$8,550
Management	$1,200
Depreciation	$3,454
Estimated sales price in 3 years	$140,000
Selling expenses	7% of selling price
Tax on sale	$7,668

    a. The buyer's initial investment will be _____.

    b. Each year's cash flow before taxes will be _____.

    c. The remaining balance at the end of 3 years will be _____.

    d. Net proceeds of sale after taxes if sold after 3 years will be _____.

8. Sarah is considering the purchase of an 8-acre tract of vacant land. Information on the expected cash flows for the purchase, ownership, and sale of the property follows:

Initial investment	$20,000
Annual after-tax cash flows	($ 6,000)
Net sales proceeds in 5 years	$80,000

    a. Determine the internal rate of return.

    b. Determine the FMRR safe rate method using 8%.

    c. Determine the FMRR borrowing rate method using 10%.

9. A.W. is contemplating the purchase of land, information on which follows:

Purchase price	$85,000
Down payment	$20,000
Balance to be financed at 8% interest with annual payments of $5,400	
There is no income from the property.	
Real estate taxes	$1,500 per year
A.W.'s tax bracket	30%
Expected after-tax net sales proceeds in 4 years	$65,000

   a. Find A.W.'s cash flow after taxes.
   b. Compute the FMRR safe rate method using 8%.
   c. Compute the FMRR borrowing rate method using 12%.

10. Jessica is considering the purchase of the following property:

Initial investment	$20,000
After-tax cash flows	
Year 1	$ 3,800
2	$ 4,200
3	($ 2,200
4	($ 3,600)
5	($ 5,600)
Net sales proceeds in 5 years	$42,000
Jessica's safe rate is 5.5%. Her borrowing rate is 9.5%.	

   a. Find her FMRR by the safe rate method (pay as you go).
   b. Find her FMRR by the borrowing rate method.

Chapter 6

MAKING DECISIONS

Everyone who has bought an investment property may tell you their techniques for how they determined the sale price. But in this chapter we will make decisions based on the collected and analyzed data. Regardless of how the information is analyzed the numbers will be viewed differently by different investors. So we are at the point where we must ask ourselves, How do we make a good, logical decision from this information that we have collected and analyzed? How do we put together an offer that will get for us the return that we desire? If we cannot get that return, then why bother buying the property? Let's take a look at the following listing and examine several different offers.

The information given will reflect the following economic conditions:

1. Interest rates between 8% and 10%
2. Low inflation rate
3. Stable economy
4. Low unemployment
5. Banks generally requiring 25% to 30% down payment for non-owner occupied investment properties.

The property is a four-unit with a garage located on the east side of Lancaster, PA.

INCOME

Unit 1: 1st floor 3-bedroom	$475 per month
Unit 2: 2nd floor 3-bedroom	$425 per month
Unit 3: 3rd floor efficiency	$265 per month
Unit 4: 3rd floor efficiency	$300 per month
Garage	$ 45 per month

EXPENSES (all expenses are yearly)	
Accounting fees	$70
Advertising	$120
Property insurance	$400
Property management	By owner
School taxes	$1,600
Municipal & county taxes	$600
Lawn care	$80
Snow removal	$80
Licenses	$20 per unit (does not include the garage)
Legal	$200
Maintenance	$500
Trash	$400
Electric	$240
Gas	$320
Oil	$1,720
Water and sewer	$825
Area vacancy rate	5%
Depreciation basis	27.5 years/straight-line
Inflation rate	2.7%
Total assessment value	$25,000
Land assessment	$1,500
Improvemnt assessment	$23,500
Typical interest rate	8.5% for a 20-year term
Owner has no existing mortgage balance.	
Currently listed for	$120,000
Reason for selling	Dissolution of partnership
Current realtor commission charge for selling	6%
Tax rate of buyer	28%

Offer 1: Full Price

Amount of down payment	30% or $36,000
Closing costs to buy	$6,000
Mortgage	Bank loan for $84,000 at 8.5% for 20 years ($728.97 per month)

Net operating income will stay the same for all examples since the expenses and the rents are not going to be changed prior to purchase. These are items that could be changed after the purchase but when you are purchasing you should never buy on potential or on what you think might happen. Buying on potential is pure speculation and the comfort level for the risk must be increased.

After preparing the APOD the NOI is $9,939.

The before-tax cash flow is $1,191 (so annual debt service is covered).

The capitalization rate based on the owner's list price is:

Cap rate = $\dfrac{\$9,939}{\$120,000} \times 100$

Cap rate = 8.3%

This would not be acceptable for most investors.

The CFA shows a mortgage balance at the end of 5 years of $74,027.

The after-tax cash flows at the end of each year are:

$1,538 $1,690 $1,945 $2,208 $2,479

If we sell in 5 years using 2.7% inflation, the new sale price should be $137,099.

Selling expenses include a 6% commission and 1% transfer tax.

Net sales proceeds are $45,632.

Using the FMRR reinvestment method with the cash flows only earning 2.7% per year:

$1,538 at 2.7% for 4 yrs. yields	$ 1,711
$1,690 at 2.7% for 3 yrs. yields	$ 1,831
$1,945 at 2.7% for 2 yrs. yields	$ 2,051
$2,208 at 2.7% for 1 yr. yields	$ 2,268
$2,479 + $45,632 equals	$48,111
	$55,972
Initial investment is $36,000 + $6,000 = $42,000.	

Calculator Steps

1. Enter 42,000, hit CHS, hit PV.
2. Enter 55,972, hit FV.
3. Enter 5, hit n.
4. Hit i.

The result is 5.9%. Yuck!

ANNUAL PROPERTY OPERATING DATA

Name: I Need to Make a Decision

Property Address: Lancaster, PA

Type of Property: 4-unit & garage

Assessed/Appraised Values

Land:	$1,500	6.00%
Improvement:	$23,500	94.00%
Personal Prop.:		0.00%
Total:	$25,000	100.00%

Date:	Offer #1	
Price:	$120,000.00	
Equity:	$ 36,000.00	30.00%
Loans:	$ 84,000.00	

Mortgage:	1st	2nd
Balance:	$ 84,000.00	$0.00
Int. Rate:	8.50%	10.50%
Term:	20	20
Payment:	$728.97	$0.00

	1	2	3	Comments
1	SCHEDULED RENTAL INCOME		$18,120	Unit #1 $475
2	Less: Vacancy and Credit Losses	5.00%	$906	Unit #2 $425
3	EFFECTIVE RENTAL INCOME		$17,214	Unit #3 $265
4	Plus: Other Income			Unit #4 $300
5	GROSS OPERATING INCOME		$17,214	Garage $ 45
	less			
6	OPERATING EXPENSES			
7	Accounting	$70		
8	Advertising	$120		
9	Property Insurance	$400		
10	Property Management	$0		by owner
11	Personal Property Taxes	$0		
12	School Taxes	$1,600		
13	Municipal & County Taxes	$600		
14	Repairs and Maintenance	$500		
15	Laundry	$0		
16	Lawn Care	$80		
17	Snow Removal	$80		
18	Legal	$200		
19	Licenses/Permits	$80		
20	Cable TV	$0		
21	Trash	$440		
22	Supplies	$0		
23	Electricity	$240		
24	Gas	$320		
25	Oil	$1,720		
26	Water and sewer	$825		
27	Telephone	$0		
28	Miscellaneous	$0		
29				
	less			
30	TOTAL OPERATING EXPENSES		$7,275	
	equals			
31	NET OPERATING INCOME		$9,939	
32	ANNUAL DEBT SERVICE		$8,748	
	equals			
33	BEFORE-TAX CASH FLOW		$1,191	

CASH FLOW ANALYSIS

Name: <u>I Need to Make a Decision</u>   Date: <u>**Offer #1**</u>

MORTGAGE DATA

	Encumbrances	Beginning Balance	Remaining Term	Interest Rate	Monthly Payment	Annual Debt
1	1st Mortgage	$84,000	20	8.50%	$728.97	$8,748
2	2nd Mortgage	$0	20	10.50%	$0.00	$0

		year 1	year 2	year 3	year 4	year 5
3	1st Mortgage Bal. (EOY)	$82,328	$80,509	$78,528	$76,373	$74,027
4	2nd Mortgage Bal. (EOY)	$0	$0	$0	$0	$0
5	Remaining Balance (EOY)	$82,328	$80,509	$78,528	$76,373	$74,027
6	Principal Paid (EOY)	$1,672	$1,820	$1,980	$2,155	$2,346
7	Total Interest (EOY)	$7,076	$6,928	$6,767	$6,592	$6,402

TAXABLE INCOME

		year 1	year 2	year 3	year 4	year 5
8	Gross Operating Income	$17,214	$17,679	$18,298	$18,938	$19,601
	less					
9	Total Operating Expense	$7,275	$7,471	$7,673	$7,880	$8,093
	equals					
10	Net Operating Income	$9,939	$10,208	$10,625	$11,058	$11,508
	less					
11	Total Interest	$7,076	$6,928	$6,767	$6,592	$6,402
	less					
12	Depreciation	$4,102	$4,102	$4,102	$4,102	$4,102
	equals					
13	TAXABLE INCOME	($1,239)	($822)	($244)	$364	$1,004

CASH FLOW AFTER TAXES

		year 1	year 2	year 3	year 4	year 5
14	Net Operating Income	$9,939	$10,207	$10,624	$11,058	$11,508
	less					
15	Annual Debt Service	$8,748	$8,748	$8,748	$8,748	$8,748
	less					
16	Capital Additions	$0	$0	$0	$0	$0
	equals					
17	Cash Flow before Taxes	$1,191	$1,459	$1,876	$2,310	$2,760
	less					
18	Tax Liability	($347)	($230)	($69)	$102	$281
	equals					
19	CASH FLOW AFTER TAXES	$1,538	$1,689	$1,945	$2,208	$2,479

Inflation rate   2.70%
Tax rate   28.00%

NET SALES PROCEEDS
Offer #1

Calculating Adjusted Cost Basis

1.	Original basis	$120,000
2.	Plus capital improvements	$0
3.	Plus selling expenses	$9,597 (6% comm. 1% transfer tax)
4.	Minus depreciation	$20,510
5.	Minus partial sales	
	Equals	
6.	Adjusted cost basis	$109,087

Calculating the Gain upon Sale

7.	Sales price	$137,099 (2.7% per year)
8.	Minus adjusted cost basis	$109,087
	Equals	
9.	Capital Gain	$28,012

Calculating the Tax on the Gain

10.	Capital gain	$28,012
11.	Times tax bracket	28.00%
	Equals	
12.	Total tax	$7,843

Calculating the Net Sales Proceeds

13.	Sales price	$137,099
14.	Minus selling expenses	$9,597
15.	Minus mortgage balances	$74,027
16.	Minus tax on gain	$7,843
	Equals	
17.	Net sales proceeds	$45,632

Offer 2: Full Price

Amount of down payment	$24,560 (This is the minimum that can be put down so that the property will carry the debt service.)
Closing costs to buy	$6,000
Mortgage	Bank loan for $95,440 at 8.5% for 20 years ($828.25 per month or $9,939 per year)

After preparing the APOD the NOI is $9,939.

The before-tax cash flow is $0 (so annual debt service is covered).

The capitalization rate based on the owner's list price is still:

$$\text{Cap rate} = \frac{\$9,939}{\$120,000} \times 100$$

Cap rate = 8.3%

The CFA shows a mortgage balance at the end of 5 years of $84,109.

The after-tax cash flows at the end of each year are:

$617 $763 $1,012 $1,268 $1,532

If we sell in 5 years using 2.7% inflation, the new sale price should be $137,099.

Selling expenses include a 6% commission and 1% transfer tax.

Net sales proceeds are $35,550.

Using the FMRR reinvestment method with the cash flows only earning 2.7% per year:

$617 at 2.7% for 4 yrs. yields	$ 686
$763 at 2.7% for 3 yrs. yields	$ 831
$1,012 at 2.7% for 2 yrs. yields	$ 1,067
$1,268 at 2.7% for 1 yr. yields	$ 1,302
$1,532 + $35,550 equals	$37,082
	$40,968

Initial investment is $24,560 + $6,000 = $30,560.

Calculator Steps

1. Enter 30,560, hit CHS, hit PV.
2. Enter 40,968, hit FV.
3. Enter 5, hit n.
4. Hit I.

The result is 6.03%. Yuck!

ANNUAL PROPERTY OPERATING DATA

Name: I Need to Make a Decision   Date: **Offer #2**

Property Address: Lancaster, PA   Price: **$120,000.00**

Type of Property: 4-unit & garage   Equity: **$ 24,560.00**   30.00%

     Loans: **$ 95,440.00**

Assessed/Appraised Values

			Mortgage:	1st	2nd
Land:	$1,500	6.00%	Balance:	$ 95,440.00	$0.00
Improvement:	$23,500	94.00%	Int. Rate:	8.50%	10.50%
Personal Prop.:		0.00%	Term:	20	20
Total:	$25,000	100.00%	Payment:	$828.25	$0.00

		1	2	3	Comments
1		SCHEDULED RENTAL INCOME		$18,120	Unit #1 $475
2		Less: Vacancy and Credit Losses	5.00%	$906	Unit #2 $425
3		EFFECTIVE RENTAL INCOME		$17,214	Unit #3 $265
4		Plus: Other Income			Unit #4 $300
5		GROSS OPERATING INCOME		$17,214	Garage $ 45
		less			
6		OPERATING EXPENSES			
7		Accounting	$70		
8		Advertising	$120		
9		Property Insurance	$400		
10		Property Management	$0		by owner
11		Personal Property Taxes	$0		
12		School Taxes	$1,600		
13		Municipal & County Taxes	$600		
14		Repairs and Maintenance	$500		
15		Laundry	$0		
16		Lawn Care	$80		
17		Snow Removal	$80		
18		Legal	$200		
19		Licenses/Permits	$80		
20		Cable TV	$0		
21		Trash	$440		
22		Supplies	$0		
23		Electricity	$240		
24		Gas	$320		
25		Oil	$1,720		
26		Water and sewer	$825		
27		Telephone	$0		
28		Miscellaneous	$0		
29					
30		TOTAL OPERATING EXPENSES		$7,275	
		equals			
31		NET OPERATING INCOME		$9,939	
		less			
32		ANNUAL DEBT SERVICE		$9,939	
		equals			
33		BEFORE-TAX CASH FLOW		$0	

CASH FLOW ANALYSIS

Name: <u>I Need to Make a Decision</u>   Date: <u>**Offer #2**</u>

MORTGAGE DATA

	Encumbrances	Beginning Balance	Remaining Term	Interest Rate	Monthly Payment	Annual Debt
1	1st Mortgage	$95,440	20	8.50%	$828.25	$9,939
2	2nd Mortgage	$0	20	10.50%	$0.00	$0

		year 1	year 2	year 3	year 4	year 5
3	1st Mortgage Bal. (EOY)	$93,541	$91,473	$89,223	$86,774	$84,109
4	2nd Mortgage Bal. (EOY)	$0	$0	$0	$0	$0
5	Remaining Balance (EOY)	$93,541	$91,473	$89,223	$86,774	$84,109
6	Principal Paid (EOY)	$1,899	$2,067	$2,250	$2,449	$2,665
7	Total Interest (EOY)	$8,040	$7,872	$7,689	$7,490	$7,274

TAXABLE INCOME

8	Gross Operating Income	$17,214	$17,679	$18,298	$18,938	$19,601
	less					
9	Total Operating Expense	$7,275	$7,471	$7,673	$7,880	$8,093
	equals					
10	Net Operating Income	$9,939	$10,208	$10,625	$11,058	$11,508
	less					
11	Total Interest	$8,040	$7,872	$7,689	$7,490	$7,274
	less					
12	Depreciation	$4,102	$4,102	$4,102	$4,102	$4,102
	equals					
13	TAXABLE INCOME	($2,203)	($1,766)	($1,166)	($534)	$132

CASH FLOW AFTER TAXES

14	Net Operating Income	$9,939	$10,208	$10,625	$11,058	$11,508
	less					
15	Annual Debt Service	$9,939	$9,939	$9,939	$9,939	$9,939
	less					
16	Capital Additions	$0	$0	$0	$0	$0
	equals					
17	Cash Flow before Taxes	($0)	$269	$686	$1,119	$1,569
	less					
18	Tax Liability	($617)	($495)	($327)	($150)	$37
	equals					
19	CASH FLOW AFTER TAXES	$617	$764	$1,013	$1,269	$1,532

Inflation rate   2.70%
Tax rate   28.00%

NET SALES PROCEEDS
Offer #2

Calculating Adjusted Cost Basis

1.	Original basis	$120,000	
2.	Plus capital improvements	$0	
3.	Plus selling expenses	$9,597	(6% comm. 1% transfer tax)
4.	Minus depreciation	$20,510	
5.	Minus partial sales		
	Equals		
6.	Adjusted cost basis	$109,087	

Calculating the Gain upon Sale

7.	Sales price	$137,099	(2.7% per year)
8.	Minus adjusted cost basis	$109,087	
	Equals		
9.	Capital Gain	$28,012	

Calculating the Tax on the Gain

10.	Capital gain	$28,012
11.	Times tax bracket	28.00%
	Equals	
12.	Total tax	$7,843

Calculating the Net Sales Proceeds

13.	Sales price	$137,099
14.	Minus selling expenses	$9,597
15.	Minus mortgage balances	$84,109
16.	Minus tax on gain	$7,843
	Equals	
17.	Net sales proceeds	$35,550

Offer 3: Full Price

Amount of down payment	$10,000
Closing costs to buy	$6,000
Mortgage	Bank loan for $90,000 at 8.5% for 20 years ($781.04 per month)
	2nd mortgage from owner for $20,000 at 8.5% for 20 yrs. ($173.56 per month)

After preparing the APOD, the NOI is $9,939.

The before-tax cash flow is (1,561) (so annual debt service is not covered).

The capitalization rate based on the owner's list price is still:

$$\text{Cap rate} = \frac{\$9,939}{\$120,000} \times 100$$

Cap rate = 8.3%

The CFA shows a mortgage balance at the end of 5 years of $96,940.

The after-tax cash flows at the end of each year are:

($556)   ($417)   ($176) $72 $326

If we sell in 5 years using 2.7% inflation, the new sale price should be $137,099.

Selling expenses include a 6% commission and 1% transfer tax.

Net sales proceeds are $22,720.

Using the FMRR reinvestment method with the cash flows only earning 2.7% per year and borrowing rate at 9% per year:

($556) at 9% for 4 yrs. yields	($ 785)
($417) at 9% for 3 yrs. yields	($ 540)
($176) at 9% for 2 yrs. yields	($ 209)
$72 at 2.7% for 1 yr. yields	$ 74
$326 + $22,720 equals	$23,046
	$21,586

Initial investment is $10,000 + $6,000 = $16,000.

Calculator Steps

1. Enter 16,000, hit CHS, hit PV.
2. Enter 21,586, hit FV.
3. Enter 5, hit n.
4. Hit i.

The result is 6.2%. Yuck!

ANNUAL PROPERTY OPERATING DATA

Name: I Need to Make a Decision

Property Address: Lancaster, PA

Type of Property: 4-unit & garage

Date: Offer #3

Price: $120,000.00

Equity: $ 10,000.00   30.00%

Loans: $110,000.00

Assessed/Appraised Values

Land:	$1,500	6.00%
Improvement:	$23,500	94.00%
Personal Prop.:		0.00%
Total:	$25,000	100.00%

Mortgage:	1st	2nd
Balance:	$ 90,000.00	$20,000.00
Int. Rate:	8.50%	10.50%
Term:	20	20
Payment:	$781.04	$173.56

	1	2	3	Comments
1	SCHEDULED RENTAL INCOME		$18,120	Unit #1 $475
2	Less: Vacancy and Credit Losses	5.00%	$906	Unit #2 $425
3	EFFECTIVE RENTAL INCOME		$17,214	Unit #3 $265
4	Plus: Other Income			Unit #4 $300
5	GROSS OPERATING INCOME		$17,214	Garage $ 45
	less			
6	OPERATING EXPENSES			
7	Accounting	$70		
8	Advertising	$120		
9	Property Insurance	$400		
10	Property Management	$0		by owner
11	Personal Property Taxes	$0		
12	School Taxes	$1,600		
13	Municipal & County Taxes	$600		
14	Repairs and Maintenance	$500		
15	Laundry	$0		
16	Lawn Care	$80		
17	Snow Removal	$80		
18	Legal	$200		
19	Licenses/Permits	$80		
20	Cable TV	$0		
21	Trash	$440		
22	Supplies	$0		
23	Electricity	$240		
24	Gas	$320		
25	Oil	$1,720		
26	Water and sewer	$825		
27	Telephone	$0		
28	Miscellaneous	$0		
29				
30	TOTAL OPERATING EXPENSES		$7,275	
	equals			
31	NET OPERATING INCOME		$9,939	
	less			
32	ANNUAL DEBT SERVICE		$11,455	
	equals			
33	BEFORE-TAX CASH FLOW		($1,516)	

CASH FLOW ANALYSIS

Name: <u>I Need to Make a Decision</u>   Date: <u>Offer #3</u>

MORTGAGE DATA

	Encumbrances	Beginning Balance	Remaining Term	Interest Rate	Monthly Payment	Annual Debt
1	1st Mortgage	$90,000	20	8.50%	$781.04	$9,372
2	2nd Mortgage	$20,000	20	8.50%	$173.56	$2,083

		year 1	year 2	year 3	year 4	year 5
3	1st Mortgage Bal. (EOY)	$88,209	$86,259	$84,137	$81,828	$79,314
4	2nd Mortgage Bal. (EOY)	$19,602	$19,169	$18,697	$18,184	$17,625
5	Remaining Balance (EOY)	$107,811	$105,428	$102,835	$100,012	$96,940
6	Principal Paid (EOY)	$2,189	$2,383	$2,593	$2,823	$3,072
7	Total Interest (EOY)	$9,266	$9,073	$8,862	$8,633	$8,383

TAXABLE INCOME

		year 1	year 2	year 3	year 4	year 5
8	Gross Operating Income	$17,214	$17,679	$18,298	$18,938	$19,601
	less					
9	Total Operating Expense	$7,275	$7,471	$7,673	$7,880	$8,093
	equals					
10	Net Operating Income	$9,939	$10,208	$10,625	$11,058	$11,508
	less					
11	Total Interest	$9,266	$9,073	$8,862	$8,633	$8,383
	less					
12	Depreciation	$4,102	$4,102	$4,102	$4,102	$4,102
	equals					
13	TAXABLE INCOME	($3,429)	($2,967)	($2,339)	($1,677)	($977)

CASH FLOW AFTER TAXES

		year 1	year 2	year 3	year 4	year 5
14	Net Operating Income	$9,939	$10,208	$10,625	$11,058	$11,508
	less					
15	Annual Debt Service	$11,455	$11,455	$11,455	$11,455	$11,455
	less					
16	Capital Additions	$0	$0	$0	$0	$0
	equals					
17	Cash Flow Before Taxes	($1,516)	($1,247)	($830)	($397)	$53
	less					
18	Tax Liability	($960)	($831)	($655)	($470)	($274)
	equals					
19	CASH FLOW AFTER TAXES	($556)	($416)	($175)	$73	$327

Inflation rate   2.70%
Tax rate   28.00%

NET SALES PROCEEDS
Offer #3

Calculating Adjusted Cost Basis

1.	Original basis	$120,000	
2.	Plus capital improvements	$0	
3.	Plus selling expenses	$9,597	(6% comm. 1% transfer tax)
4.	Minus depreciation	$20,510	
5.	Minus partial sales		
	Equals		
6.	Adjusted cost basis	$109,087	

Calculating the Gain upon Sale

7.	Sales price	$137,099	(2.7% per year)
8.	Minus adjusted cost basis	$109,087	
	Equals		
9.	Capital Gain	$28,012	

Calculating the Tax on the Gain

10.	Capital gain	$28,012
11.	Times tax bracket	28.00%
	Equals	
12.	Total tax	$7,843

Calculating the Net Sales Proceeds

13.	Sales price	$137,099
14.	Minus selling expenses	$9,597
15.	Minus mortgage balances	$96,939
16.	Minus tax on gain	$7,843
	Equals	
17.	Net sales proceeds	$22,720

Offer 4: Full Price (Installment Sale)

Amount of down payment	$10,000
Closing costs to buy	To be paid 5 years down the road when property is resold. Since the buyer must pay off the seller and get the deed before reselling there will be some closing costs but not as high as if the buyer were to purchase the property up front with a bank loan. This buyer is hoping to flip the property on the same day, in other words, buy it and sell it on the same day. Let's estimate closing costs to be $3,200.
Mortgage	Loan from seller for $110,000 at 9.0%* for 20 years ($989.70 per month)

*Seller is a tough negotiator.

After preparing the APOD, the NOI is $9,939.

The before-tax cash flow is $1,937 (so annual debt service is not covered).

The capitalization rate based on the owner's list price is still:

$$\text{Cap rate} = \frac{\$9,939}{\$120,000} \times 100$$

Cap rate = 8.3%

The CFA shows a mortgage balance at the end of 5 years of $97,578.

The after-tax cash flows at the end of each year are:

($823)   ($684)   ($443)   ($196) $57

If we sell in 5 years using 2.7% inflation, the new sale price should be $137,099.

Selling expenses include a 6% commission and 1% transfer tax.

Net sales proceeds are $22,081.

Using the FMRR reinvestment method with the cash flows only earning 2.7% per year and borrowing rate at 9% per year:

($823) at 9% for 4 yrs. yields	($ 1,162)
($684) at 9% for 3 yrs. yields	($ 886)
($443) at 9% for 2 yrs. yields	($ 526)
($196) at 9% for 1 yr. yields	($ 214)
$57 + $22,081 equals	$22,138
	$19,350
But we have to pay closing costs of	$ 3,200
	$16,150

Initial investment is $10,000.

Calculator Steps

1. Enter 10,000, hit CHS, hit PV.
2. Enter 16,150, hit FV.
3. Enter 5, hit n.
4. Hit i.

The result is 10.1%. This is getting better!

ANNUAL PROPERTY OPERATING DATA

Name: I Need to Make a Decision
Property Address: Lancaster, PA
Type of Property: 4-unit & garage

Date: **Offer #4**
Price: **$120,000.00**
Equity: **$ 10,000.00**
Loans: **$110,000.00**

Assessed/Appraised Values

Land:	$1,500	6.00%
Improvement:	$23,500	94.00%
Personal Prop.:		0.00%
Total:	$25,000	100.00%

Mortgage:	1st	2nd
Balance:	$110,000.00	
Int. Rate:	9.00%	8.50%
Term:	20	20
Payment:	$989.70	$0.00

		1	2	3	Comments
1		SCHEDULED RENTAL INCOME		$18,120	Unit #1 $475
2		Less: Vacancy and Credit Losses	5.00%	$906	Unit #2 $425
3		EFFECTIVE RENTAL INCOME		$17,214	Unit #3 $265
4		Plus: Other Income			Unit #4 $300
5		GROSS OPERATING INCOME		$17,214	Garage $ 45
		less			
6		OPERATING EXPENSES			
7		Accounting	$70		
8		Advertising	$120		
9		Property Insurance	$400		
10		Property Management	$0		by owner
11		Personal Property Taxes	$0		
12		School Taxes	$1,600		
13		Municipal & County Taxes	$600		
14		Repairs and Maintenance	$500		
15		Laundry	$0		
16		Lawn Care	$80		
17		Snow Removal	$80		
18		Legal	$200		
19		Licenses/Permits	$80		
20		Cable TV	$0		
21		Trash	$440		
22		Supplies	$0		
23		Electricity	$240		
24		Gas	$320		
25		Oil	$1,720		
26		Water and sewer	$825		
27		Telephone	$0		
28		Miscellaneous	$0		
29					
30		TOTAL OPERATING EXPENSES		$7,275	
		equals			
31		NET OPERATING INCOME		$9,939	
		less			
32		ANNUAL DEBT SERVICE		$11,876	
		equals			
33		BEFORE-TAX CASH FLOW		($1,937)	

CASH FLOW ANALYSIS

Name: <u>I Need to Make a Decision</u>   Date: <u>Offer #4</u>

MORTGAGE DATA

	Encumbrances	Beginning Balance	Remaining Term	Interest Rate	Monthly Payment	Annual Debt
1	1st Mortgage	$110,000	20	9.00%	$989.70	$11,876
2	2nd Mortgage	$0	20	8.50%	$0.00	$0

		year 1	year 2	year 3	year 4	year 5
3	1st Mortgage Bal. (EOY)	$107,940	$105,687	$103,222	$100,526	$97,578
4	2nd Mortgage Bal. (EOY)	$0	$0	$0	$0	$0
5	Remaining Balance (EOY)	$107,940	$105,687	$103,222	$100,526	$97,578
6	Principal Paid (EOY)	$2,060	$2,253	$2,465	$2,696	$2,949
7	Total Interest (EOY)	$9,816	$9,623	$9,412	$9,181	$8,928

TAXABLE INCOME

		year 1	year 2	year 3	year 4	year 5
8	Gross Operating Income	$17,214	$17,679	$18,298	$18,938	$19,601
	less					
9	Total Operating Expense	$7,275	$7,471	$7,673	$7,880	$8,093
	equals					
10	Net Operating Income	$9,939	$10,208	$10,625	$11,058	$11,508
	less					
11	Total Interest	$9,816	$9,623	$9,412	$9,181	$8,928
	less					
12	Depreciation	$4,102	$4,102	$4,102	$4,102	$4,102
	equals					
13	TAXABLE INCOME	($3,979)	($3,517)	($2,889)	($2,225)	($1,522)

CASH FLOW AFTER TAXES

		year 1	year 2	year 3	year 4	year 5
14	Net Operating Income	$9,939	$10,208	$10,625	$11,058	$11,508
	less					
15	Annual Debt Service	$11,876	$11,876	$11,876	$11,876	$11,876
	less					
16	Capital Additions	$0	$0	$0	$0	$0
	equals					
17	Cash Flow before Taxes	($1,937)	($1,668)	($1,251)	($818)	($368)
	less					
18	Tax Liability	($1,114)	($985)	($809)	($623)	($426)
	equals					
19	CASH FLOW AFTER TAXES	($823)	($683)	($442)	($195)	$58

Inflation rate   2.70%
Tax rate   28.00%

NET SALES PROCEEDS
Offer #4

Calculating Adjusted Cost Basis

1.	Original basis	$120,000	
2.	Plus capital improvements	$0	
3.	Plus selling expenses	$9,597	(6% comm. 1% transfer tax)
4.	Minus depreciation	$20,510	
5.	Minus partial sales		
	Equals		
6.	Adjusted cost basis	$109,087	

Calculating the Gain upon Sale

7.	Sales price	$137,099	(2.7% per year)
8.	Minus adjusted cost basis	$109,087	
	Equals		
9.	Capital Gain	$28,012	

Calculating the Tax on the Gain

10.	Capital gain	$28,012
11.	Times tax bracket	28.00%
	Equals	
12.	Total tax	$7,843

Calculating the Net Sales Proceeds

13.	Sales price	$137,099
14.	Minus selling expenses	$9,597
15.	Minus mortgage balances	$97,538
16.	Minus tax on gain	$7,843
	Equals	
17.	Net sales proceeds	$22,121

Offer 5: $110,000—Pay Attention
(This is below asking price)

Amount of down payment	$20,000
Closing costs to buy	$6,000
Mortgage	Bank loan for $90,000 at 8.5% for 20 years ($781.04 per month)

After preparing the APOD, the NOI is $9,939.

The before-tax cash flow is $567 (so annual debt service is covered).

The capitalization rate based on the owner's list price is still:

$$\text{Cap rate} = \frac{\$9,939}{\$120,000} \times 100$$

Cap rate = 8.3%

The CFA shows a mortgage balance at the end of 5 years of $79,314.

The after-tax cash flows at the end of each year are:

$959 $1,108 $1,360 $1,619 $1,886

If we sell in 5 years using 2.7% inflation, the new sale price should be $125,674. (Remember, we are buying it for $110,000.)

This also affects the depreciation per year ($3,760).

Selling expenses include a 6% commission and 1% transfer tax.

Net sales proceeds are $30,373.

Using the FMRR reinvestment method with the cash flows only earning 2.7% per year:

$959 at 2.7% for 4 yrs. yields	$ 1,067
$1,108 at 2.7% for 3 yrs. yields	$ 1,200
$1,360 at 2.7% for 2 yrs. yields	$ 1,434
$1,619 at 2.7% for 1 yr. yields	$ 1,662
$1,886 + $30,373 equals	$32,259
	$37,622

Initial investment is $20,000 + $6,000 = $26,000.

Calculator Steps

1. Enter 26,000, hit CHS, hit PV.
2. Enter 37,622, hit FV.
3. Enter 5, hit n.
4. Hit i.

The result is 7.67%. This shows that not all lower offers generate higher returns!

ANNUAL PROPERTY OPERATING DATA

Name: **I Need to Make a Decision**

Property Address: Lancaster, PA

Type of Property: 4-unit & garage

Date:	Offer #5
Price:	$110,000.00
Equity:	$ 20,000.00
Loans:	$ 90,000.00

Assessed/Appraised Values

Land:	$1,500	6.00%
Improvement:	$23,500	94.00%
Personal Prop.:		0.00%
Total:	$25,000	100.00%

Mortgage:	1st	2nd
Balance:	$ 90,000.00	
Int. Rate:	8.50%	8.50%
Term:	20	20
Payment:	$781.04	$0.00

		1	2	3	Comments
1	SCHEDULED RENTAL INCOME			$18,120	Unit #1 $475
2	Less: Vacancy and Credit Losses		5.00%	$906	Unit #2 $425
3	EFFECTIVE RENTAL INCOME			$17,214	Unit #3 $265
4	Plus: Other Income				Unit #4 $300
5	GROSS OPERATING INCOME			$17,214	Garage $ 45
	less				
6	OPERATING EXPENSES				
7	Accounting		$70		
8	Advertising		$120		
9	Property Insurance		$400		
10	Property Management		$0		by owner
11	Personal Property Taxes		$0		
12	School Taxes		$1,600		
13	Municipal & County Taxes		$600		
14	Repairs and Maintenance		$500		
15	Laundry		$0		
16	Lawn Care		$80		
17	Snow Removal		$80		
18	Legal		$200		
19	Licenses/Permits		$80		
20	Cable TV		$0		
21	Trash		$440		
22	Supplies		$0		
23	Electricity		$240		
24	Gas		$320		
25	Oil		$1,720		
26	Water and sewer		$825		
27	Telephone		$0		
28	Miscellaneous		$0		
29					
30	TOTAL OPERATING EXPENSES			$7,275	
	equals				
31	NET OPERATING INCOME			$9,939	
	less				
32	ANNUAL DEBT SERVICE			$9,372	
	equals				
33	BEFORE-TAX CASH FLOW			$567	

CASH FLOW ANALYSIS

Name: <u>I Need to Make a Decision</u>   Date: <u>Offer #5</u>

MORTGAGE DATA

	Encumbrances	Beginning Balance	Remaining Term	Interest Rate	Monthly Payment	Annual Debt
1	1st Mortgage	$90,000	20	8.50%	$781.04	$9,372
2	2nd Mortgage	$0	20	8.50%	$0.00	$0

		year 1	year 2	year 3	year 4	year 5
3	1st Mortgage Bal. (EOY)	$88,209	$86,259	$84,137	$81,828	$79,314
4	2nd Mortgage Bal. (EOY)	$0	$0	$0	$0	$0
5	Remaining Balance (EOY)	$88,209	$86,259	$84,137	$81,828	$79,314
6	Principal Paid (EOY)	$1,791	$1,950	$2,122	$2,309	$2,514
7	Total Interest (EOY)	$7,581	$7,423	$7,251	$7,063	$6,859

TAXABLE INCOME

		year 1	year 2	year 3	year 4	year 5
8	Gross Operating Income	$17,214	$17,679	$18,298	$18,938	$19,601
	less					
9	Total Operating Expense	$7,275	$7,471	$7,673	$7,880	$8,093
	equals					
10	Net Operating Income	$9,939	$10,208	$10,625	$11,058	$11,508
	less					
11	Total Interest	$7,581	$7,423	$7,251	$7,063	$6,859
	less					
12	Depreciation	$3,760	$3,760	$3,760	$3,760	$3,760
	equals					
13	TAXABLE INCOME	($1,402)	($975)	($386)	$235	$889

CASH FLOW AFTER TAXES

		year 1	year 2	year 3	year 4	year 5
14	Net Operating Income	$9,939	$10,208	$10,625	$11,058	$11,508
	less					
15	Annual Debt Service	$9,372	$9,372	$9,372	$9,372	$9,372
	less					
16	Capital Additions	$0	$0	$0	$0	$0
	equals					
17	Cash Flow Before Taxes	$567	$836	$1,253	$1,686	$2,136
	less					
18	Tax Liability	($393)	($273)	($108)	$66	$249
	equals					
19	CASH FLOW AFTER TAXES	$960	$1,109	$1,361	$1,620	$1,887

Inflation rate   2.70%
Tax rate   28.00%

NET SALES PROCEEDS
Offer #5

Calculating Adjusted Cost Basis

1.	Original basis	$110,000	
2.	Plus capital improvements	$0	
3.	Plus selling expenses	$8,797	(6% comm. 1% transfer tax)
4.	Minus depreciation	$18,800	
5.	Minus partial sales		
	Equals		
6.	Adjusted cost basis	$99,997	

Calculating the Gain upon Sale

7.	Sales price	$125,674	(2.7% per year)
8.	Minus adjusted cost basis	$99,997	
	Equals		
9.	Capital Gain	$25,677	

Calculating the Tax on the Gain

10.	Capital gain	$25,677
11.	Times tax bracket	28.00%
	Equals	
12.	Total tax	$7,190

Calculating the Net Sales Proceeds

13.	Sales price	$125,674
14.	Minus selling expenses	$8,797
15.	Minus mortgage balances	$79,314
16.	Minus tax on gain	$7,190
	Equals	
17.	Net sales proceeds	$30,373

Offer 6: $110,000—Let's Try This Again

Amount of down payment	$30,000
Closing costs to buy	$6,000
Mortgage	Bank loan for $80,000 at 8.0%* for 20 years ($669.15 per month)

*We got a better deal at the bank.

After preparing the APOD, the NOI is $9,939.

The before-tax cash flow is $1,909 (so annual debt service is covered).

The capitalization rate based on the owner's list price is still:

$$\text{Cap rate} = \frac{\$9,939}{\$120,000} \times 100$$

Cap rate = 8.3%

The CFA shows a mortgage balance at the end of 5 years of $70,020.

The after-tax cash flows at the end of each year are:

$1,954 $2,108 $2,366 $2,631 $2,906

If we sell in 5 years using 2.7% inflation, the new sale price should be $125,674. (Remember, we are buying it for $110,000.)

This also affects the depreciation per year ($3,760).

Selling expenses include a 6% commission and 1% transfer tax.

Net sales proceeds are $39,667.

Using the FMRR reinvestment method with the cash flows only earning 2.7% per year:

$1,954 at 2.7% for 4 yrs. yields	$ 2,173
$2,108 at 2.7% for 3 yrs. yields	$ 2,283
$2,366 at 2.7% for 2 yrs. yields	$ 2,495
$2,631 at 2.7% for 1 yr. yields	$ 2,702
$2,906 + $39,667 equals	$42,573
	$52,226

Initial investment is $30,000 + $6,000 = $36,000.

Calculator Steps

1. Enter 36,000, hit CHS, hit PV.
2. Enter 52,226, hit FV.
3. Enter 5, hit n.
4. Hit i.

The result is 7.7%. This is just not going to work!

ANNUAL PROPERTY OPERATING DATA

Name: I Need to Make a Decision

Property Address: Lancaster, PA

Type of Property: 4 unit & garage

Assessed/Appraised Values

Land:	$1,500	6.00%
Improvement:	$23,500	94.00%
Personal Prop.:		0.00%
Total:	$25,000	100.00%

Date: Offer #6

Price: $110,000.00

Equity: $ 30,000.00

Loans: $ 80,000.00

Mortgage:	1st	2nd
Balance:	$ 80,000.00	
Int. Rate:	8.00%	8.50%
Term:	20	20
Payment:	$669.15	$0.00

	1	2	3	Comments
1	SCHEDULED RENTAL INCOME		$18,120	Unit #1 $475
2	Less: Vacancy and Credit Losses	5.00%	$906	Unit #2 $425
3	EFFECTIVE RENTAL INCOME		$17,214	Unit #3 $265
4	Plus: Other Income			Unit #4 $300
5	GROSS OPERATING INCOME		$17,214	Garage $ 45
	less			
6	OPERATING EXPENSES			
7	Accounting	$70		
8	Advertising	$120		
9	Property Insurance	$400		
10	Property Management	$0		by owner
11	Personal Property Taxes	$0		
12	School Taxes	$1,600		
13	Municipal & County Taxes	$600		
14	Repairs and Maintenance	$500		
15	Laundry	$0		
16	Lawn Care	$80		
17	Snow Removal	$80		
18	Legal	$200		
19	Licenses/Permits	$80		
20	Cable TV	$0		
21	Trash	$440		
22	Supplies	$0		
23	Electricity	$240		
24	Gas	$320		
25	Oil	$1,720		
26	Water and sewer	$825		
27	Telephone	$0		
28	Miscellaneous	$0		
29				
30	TOTAL OPERATING EXPENSES		$7,275	
	equals			
31	NET OPERATING INCOME		$9,939	
	less			
32	ANNUAL DEBT SERVICE		$8,030	
	equals			
33	BEFORE-TAX CASH FLOW		$1,909	

CASH FLOW ANALYSIS

Name: <u>I Need to Make a Decision</u>   Date: <u>**Offer #6**</u>

MORTGAGE DATA

	Encumbrances	Beginning Balance	Remaining Term	Interest Rate	Monthly Payment	Annual Debt
1	1st Mortgage	$80,000	20	8.00%	$669.15	$8,030
2	2nd Mortgage	$0	20	8.50%	$0.00	$0

		year 1	year 2	year 3	year 4	year 5
3	1st Mortgage Bal. (EOY)	$78,309	$76,478	$74,495	$72,347	$70,020
4	2nd Mortgage Bal. (EOY)	$0	$0	$0	$0	$0
5	Remaining Balance (EOY)	$78,309	$76,478	$74,495	$72,347	$70,020
6	Principal Paid (EOY)	$1,691	$1,831	$1,983	$2,148	$2,326
7	Total Interest (EOY)	$6,339	$6,199	$6,047	$5,882	$5,704

TAXABLE INCOME

		year 1	year 2	year 3	year 4	year 5
8	Gross Operating Income	$17,214	$17,679	$18,298	$18,938	$19,601
	less					
9	Total Operating Expense	$7,275	$7,471	$7,673	$7,880	$8,093
	equals					
10	Net Operating Income	$9,939	$10,208	$10,625	$11,058	$11,508
	less					
11	Total Interest	$6,339	$6,199	$6,047	$5,882	$5,704
	less					
12	Depreciation	$3,760	$3,760	$3,760	$3,760	$3,760
	equals					
13	TAXABLE INCOME	($160)	$249	$818	$1,416	$2,044

CASH FLOW AFTER TAXES

		year 1	year 2	year 3	year 4	year 5
14	Net Operating Income	$9,939	$10,208	$10,625	$11,058	$11,508
	less					
15	Annual Debt Service	$8,030	$8,030	$8,030	$8,030	$8,030
	less					
16	Capital Additions	$0	$0	$0	$0	$0
	equals					
17	Cash Flow before Taxes	$1,909	$2,178	$2,595	$3,028	$3,478
	less					
18	Tax Liability	($45)	$70	$229	$396	$572
	equals					
19	CASH FLOW AFTER TAXES	$1,954	$2,108	$2,366	$2,632	$2,906

Inflation rate   2.70%
Tax rate   28.00%

NET SALES PROCEEDS
Offer #6

Calculating Adjusted Cost Basis

1.	Original basis	$110,000	
2.	Plus capital improvements	$0	
3.	Plus selling expenses	$8,797	(6% comm. 1% transfer tax)
4.	Minus depreciation	$18,800	
5.	Minus partial sales		
	Equals		
6.	Adjusted cost basis	$99,997	

Calculating the Gain upon Sale

7.	Sales price	$125,674	(2.7% per year)
8.	Minus adjusted cost basis	$99,997	
	Equals		
9.	Capital Gain	$25,677	

Calculating the Tax on the Gain

10.	Capital gain	$25,677
11.	Times tax bracket	28.00%
	Equals	
12.	Total tax	$7,190

Calculating the Net Sales Proceeds

13.	Sales price	$125,674
14.	Minus selling expenses	$8,797
15.	Minus mortgage balances	$70,020
16.	Minus tax on gain	$7,190
	Equals	
17.	Net sales proceeds	$39,667

Offer 7: $115,000—Pay Attention
(Offer changed again)

Amount of down payment	$20,000
Closing costs to buy	Seller to pay closing costs.
Mortgage	Bank loan for $95,000 at 8.0% for 20 years ($794.62 per month)

After preparing the APOD, the NOI is $9,939.

The before-tax cash flow is $404 (so annual debt service is covered).

The capitalization rate based on the owner's list price is still:

$$\text{Cap rate} = \frac{\$9,939}{\$120,000} \times 100$$

Cap rate = 8.3%

The CFA shows a mortgage balance at the end of 5 years of $83,149.

The after-tax cash flows at the end of each year are:

$829 $976 $1,225 $1,482 $1,747

If we sell in 5 years using 2.7% inflation, the new sale price should be $131,386. (Remember, we are buying it for $115,000.)

This also affects the depreciation per year ($3,931).

Selling expenses include a 6% commission and 1% transfer tax.

Net sales proceeds are $31,524.

Using the FMRR reinvestment method with the cash flows only earning 2.7% per year:

$829 at 2.7% for 4 yrs. yields	$ 922
$976 at 2.7% for 3 yrs. yields	$ 1,057
$1,225 at 2.7% for 2 yrs. yields	$ 1,292
$1,482 at 2.7% for 1 yr. yields	$ 1,522
$1,747 + $31,524 equals	$33,271
	$38,064

Initial investment is $20,000.

Calculator Steps

1. Enter 20,000, hit CHS, hit PV.
2. Enter 38,064, hit FV.
3. Enter 5, hit n.
4. Hit i.

The result is 13.7%. See what happens when you hold on to your cash and use opm!

ANNUAL PROPERTY OPERATING DATA

Name: I Need to Make a Decision

Property Address: Lancaster, PA

Type of Property: 4-unit & garage

Date:	Offer #7
Price:	$115,000.00
Equity:	$ 20,000.00
Loans:	$ 95,000.00

Assessed/Appraised Values

			Mortgage:	1st	2nd
Land:	$1,500	6.00%	Balance:	$ 95,000.00	
Improvement:	$23,500	94.00%	Int. Rate:	8.00%	8.50%
Personal Prop.:		0.00%	Term:	20	20
Total:	$25,000	100.00%	Payment:	$794.62	$0.00

		1	2	3	Comments
1		SCHEDULED RENTAL INCOME		$18,120	Unit #1 $475
2		Less: Vacancy and Credit Losses	5.00%	$906	Unit #2 $425
3		EFFECTIVE RENTAL INCOME		$17,214	Unit #3 $265
4		Plus: Other Income			Unit #4 $300
5		GROSS OPERATING INCOME		$17,214	Garage $ 45
		less			
6		OPERATING EXPENSES			
7		Accounting	$70		
8		Advertising	$120		
9		Property Insurance	$400		
10		Property Management	$0		by owner
11		Personal Property Taxes	$0		
12		School Taxes	$1,600		
13		Municipal & County Taxes	$600		
14		Repairs and Maintenance	$500		
15		Laundry	$0		
16		Lawn Care	$80		
17		Snow Removal	$80		
18		Legal	$200		
19		Licenses/Permits	$80		
20		Cable TV	$0		
21		Trash	$440		
22		Supplies	$0		
23		Electricity	$240		
24		Gas	$320		
25		Oil	$1,720		
26		Water and sewer	$825		
27		Telephone	$0		
28		Miscellaneous	$0		
29					
30		TOTAL OPERATING EXPENSES		$7,275	
		equals			
31		NET OPERATING INCOME		$9,939	
		less			
32		ANNUAL DEBT SERVICE		$9,535	
		equals			
33		BEFORE-TAX CASH FLOW		$404	

CASH FLOW ANALYSIS

Name: <u>I Need to Make a Decision</u>   Date: <u>**Offer #7**</u>

MORTGAGE DATA

	Encumbrances	Beginning Balance	Remaining Term	Interest Rate	Monthly Payment	Annual Debt
1	1st Mortgage	$95,000	20	8.00%	$794.62	$9,535
2	2nd Mortgage	$0	20	8.50%	$0.00	$0

		year 1	year 2	year 3	year 4	year 5
3	1st Mortgage Bal. (EOY)	$92,992	$90,817	$88,462	$85,912	$83,149
4	2nd Mortgage Bal. (EOY)	$0	$0	$0	$0	$0
5	Remaining Balance (EOY)	$92,992	$90,817	$88,462	$85,912	$83,149
6	Principal Paid (EOY)	$2,008	$2,175	$2,355	$2,551	$2,762
7	Total Interest (EOY)	$7,527	$7,361	$7,180	$6,985	$6,773

TAXABLE INCOME

		year 1	year 2	year 3	year 4	year 5
8	Gross Operating Income	$17,214	$17,679	$18,298	$18,938	$19,601
	less					
9	Total Operating Expense	$7,275	$7,471	$7,673	$7,880	$8,093
	equals					
10	Net Operating Income	$9,939	$10,208	$10,625	$11,058	$11,508
	less					
11	Total Interest	$7,527	$7,361	$7,180	$6,985	$6,773
	less					
12	Depreciation	$3,931	$3,931	$3,931	$3,931	$3,931
	equals					
13	TAXABLE INCOME	($1,519)	($1,084)	($486)	$142	$804

CASH FLOW AFTER TAXES

		year 1	year 2	year 3	year 4	year 5
14	Net Operating Income	$9,939	$10,208	$10,625	$11,058	$11,508
	less					
15	Annual Debt Service	$9,535	$9,535	$9,535	$9,535	$9,535
	less					
16	Capital Additions	$0	$0	$0	$0	$0
	equals					
17	Cash Flow Before Taxes	$404	$673	$1,090	$1,523	$1,973
	less					
18	Tax Liability	($425)	($304)	($136)	$40	$225
	equals					
19	CASH FLOW AFTER TAXES	$829	$977	$1,226	$1,483	$1,748

Inflation rate   2.70%
Tax rate   28.00%

NET SALES PROCEEDS
Offer #7

Calculating Adjusted Cost Basis

1.	Original basis	$115,000
2.	Plus capital improvements	$0
3.	Plus selling expenses	$9,197 (6% comm. 1% transfer tax)
4.	Minus depreciation	$19,655
5.	Minus partial sales	
	Equals	
6.	Adjusted cost basis	**$104,542**

Calculating the Gain upon Sale

7.	Sales price	$131,386 (2.7% per year)
8.	Minus adjusted cost basis	$104,542
	Equals	
9.	Capital Gain	**$26,844**

Calculating the Tax on the Gain

10.	Capital gain	$26,844
11.	Times tax bracket	28.00%
	Equals	
12.	Total tax	$7,516

Calculating the Net Sales Proceeds

13.	Sales price	$131,386
14.	Minus selling expenses	$9,197
15.	Minus mortgage balances	$83,149
16.	Minus tax on gain	$7,516
	Equals	
17.	Net sales proceeds	$31,524

Offer 8: $110,000—Purchase Money Mortgage

Amount of down payment	$10,000
Closing costs to buy	$1,000 (Money is being borrowed from the owner—no need for appraisal, points, lawyer fees, etc. Have seller pay the transfer taxes.)
Mortgage	Seller loan for $100,000 at 8.0% for 20 years ($836.44 per month)

This requires explanation to the owner who will receive $10,038 each year until the mortgage is called. In this example we are selling in 5 years.

This means seller has income and pays taxes only on what is received, and avoids the big hit from the IRS from cashing out.

At the end of 5 years, he would have received:

	$10,000	(down payment)
	$50,190	(monthly payments)
	$87,526	(mortgage balance)
Total	$147,716	

After preparing the APOD, the NOI is $9,939.

The before-tax cash flow is ($498) (so annual debt service is *not* covered).

The capitalization rate based on the owner's list price is still:

$$\text{Cap rate} = \frac{\$9,939}{\$120,000} \times 100$$

Cap rate = 8.3%

The CFA shows a mortgage balance at the end of 5 years of $87,526.

The after-tax cash flows at the end of each year are:

$390 $534 $781 $1,036 $1,297

If we sell in 5 years using 2.7% inflation, the new sale price should be $125,674. (Remember, we are buying it for $110,000.)

This also affects the depreciation per year ($3,760).

Selling expenses include a 6% commission and 1% transfer tax.

Net sales proceeds are $22,161.

Using the FMRR reinvestment method with the cash flows only earning 2.7% per year:

$390 at 2.7% for 4 yrs. yields	$ 433
$534 at 2.7% for 3 yrs. yields	$ 578
$781 at 2.7% for 2 yrs. yields	$ 824
$1,036 at 2.7% for 1 yr. yields	$ 1,064
$1,297 + $22,161 equals	$23,458
	$26,357

Initial investment is $10,000 + $1,000 = $11,000.

1. Enter 11,000, hit CHS, hit PV.
2. Enter 26,357, hit FV.
3. Enter 5, hit n.
4. Hit i.

The result is 19.1%. Type and sign this agreement now!

ANNUAL PROPERTY OPERATING DATA

Name: I Need to Make a Decision
Property Address: Lancaster, PA
Type of Property: 4-unit & garage

Date:	Offer #8	
Price:	$110,000.00	
Equity:	$ 10,000.00	
Loans:	$100,000.00	

Assessed/Appraised Values

Land:	$1,500	6.00%
Improvement:	$23,500	94.00%
Personal Prop.:		0.00%
Total:	$25,000	100.00%

Mortgage:	1st	2nd
Balance:	$100,000.00	
Int. Rate:	8.00%	8.50%
Term:	20	20
Payment:	$836.44	$0.00

		1	2	3	Comments
1	SCHEDULED RENTAL INCOME			$18,120	Unit #1 $475
2	Less: Vacancy and Credit Losses		5.00%	$906	Unit #2 $425
3	EFFECTIVE RENTAL INCOME			$17,214	Unit #3 $265
4	Plus: Other Income				Unit #4 $300
5	GROSS OPERATING INCOME			$17,214	Garage $ 45
	less				
6	OPERATING EXPENSES				
7	Accounting		$70		
8	Advertising		$120		
9	Property Insurance		$400		
10	Property Management		$0		by owner
11	Personal Property Taxes		$0		
12	School Taxes		$1,600		
13	Municipal & County Taxes		$600		
14	Repairs and Maintenance		$500		
15	Laundry		$0		
16	Lawn Care		$80		
17	Snow Removal		$80		
18	Legal		$200		
19	Licenses/Permits		$80		
20	Cable TV		$0		
21	Trash		$440		
22	Supplies		$0		
23	Electricity		$240		
24	Gas		$320		
25	Oil		$1,720		
26	Water and sewer		$825		
27	Telephone		$0		
28	Miscellaneous		$0		
29					
30	TOTAL OPERATING EXPENSES			$7,275	
	equals				
31	NET OPERATING INCOME			$9,939	
	less				
32	ANNUAL DEBT SERVICE			$10,037	
	equals				
33	BEFORE-TAX CASH FLOW			($98)	

CASH FLOW ANALYSIS

Name: <u>I Need to Make a Decision</u>   Date: <u>Offer #8</u>

MORTGAGE DATA

	Encumbrances	Beginning Balance	Remaining Term	Interest Rate	Monthly Payment	Annual Debt
1	1st Mortgage	$100,000	20	8.00%	$836.44	$10,037
2	2nd Mortgage	$0	20	8.50%	$0.00	$0

		year 1	year 2	year 3	year 4	year 5
3	1st Mortgage Bal. (EOY)	$97,886	$95,597	$93,118	$90,433	$87,526
4	2nd Mortgage Bal. (EOY)	$0	$0	$0	$0	$0
5	Remaining Balance (EOY)	$97,886	$95,597	$93,118	$90,433	$87,526
6	Principal Paid (EOY)	$2,114	$2,289	$2,479	$2,685	$2,908
7	Total Interest (EOY)	$7,924	$7,748	$7,558	$7,352	$7,130

TAXABLE INCOME

		year 1	year 2	year 3	year 4	year 5
8	Gross Operating Income	$17,214	$17,679	$18,298	$18,938	$19,601
	less					
9	Total Operating Expense	$7,275	$7,471	$7,673	$7,880	$8,093
	equals					
10	Net Operating Income	$9,939	$10,208	$10,625	$11,058	$11,508
	less					
11	Total Interest	$7,924	$7,748	$7,558	$7,352	$7,130
	less					
12	Depreciation	$3,760	$3,760	$3,760	$3,760	$3,760
	equals					
13	TAXABLE INCOME	($1,745)	($1,300)	($693)	($54)	$618

CASH FLOW AFTER TAXES

		year 1	year 2	year 3	year 4	year 5
14	Net Operating Income	$9,939	$10,208	$10,625	$11,058	$11,508
	less					
15	Annual Debt Service	$10,037	$10,037	$10,037	$10,037	$10,037
	less					
16	Capital Additions	$0	$0	$0	$0	$0
	equals					
17	Cash Flow Before Taxes	($98)	$171	$588	$1,021	$1,471
	less					
18	Tax Liability	($488)	($364)	($194)	($15)	$173
	equals					
19	CASH FLOW AFTER TAXES	$390	$535	$782	$1,036	$1,298

Inflation rate   2.70%
Tax rate   28.00%

NET SALES PROCEEDS
Offer #8

Calculating Adjusted Cost Basis

1.	Original basis	$110,000
2.	Plus capital improvements	$0
3.	Plus selling expenses	$8,797 (6% comm. 1% transfer tax)
4.	Minus depreciation	$18,800
5.	Minus partial sales	
	Equals	
6.	Adjusted cost basis	$99,997

Calculating the Gain upon Sale

7.	Sales price	$125,674 (2.7% per year)
8.	Minus adjusted cost basis	$99,997
	Equals	
9.	Capital Gain	$25,677

Calculating the Tax on the Gain

10.	Capital gain	$25,677
11.	Times tax bracket	28.00%
	Equals	
12.	Total tax	$7,190

Calculating the Net Sales Proceeds

13.	Sales price	$125,674
14.	Minus selling expenses	$8,797
15.	Minus mortgage balances	$87,526
16.	Minus tax on gain	$7,190
	Equals	
17.	Net sales proceeds	$22,161

Answer Key

Answers to Problem Set 1

1. $P = \dfrac{I}{RT}$

    $P = \dfrac{\$70}{(.135)(30/360)}$

    $P = \dfrac{(\$70)(360)}{(.135)(30)}$

    $P = \$6,222.22$

2. $P = \dfrac{\$150}{(.085)(30/365)}$

    $P = \$21,470.59$

3. $R = \dfrac{I}{PT}$

    $R = \dfrac{\$23.28}{(\$1,898)(.25)}$

    $R = .04924$

    $R = 4.9\%$

4. $R = \dfrac{\$6.84}{(\$130.80)(10/365)}$

    $R = 1.90872$

    $R = 190.87\%$

5. $T = \dfrac{I}{PR}$

    $T = \dfrac{\$239.28}{(\$8,700)(.095)}$

    $T = .289510$ years

    $T = (.289510)(360)$

    $T = 104$ days

6. $T = \dfrac{\$31.03}{(\$1,550)(.125)}$

    $T = .16015$ years

    $T = (.16015)(365)$

    $T = 59$ days

7. **a.** $3,795 - $755 = $3,040

   b. $I = ($3,040)(.1021)(2)$
   $I = 620.77

   c. $3,040 + $620.77 = $3,660.77

   d. $\dfrac{$3,660.77}{24} = 152.53

   e. $\dfrac{$620.77}{$3,040} \times 100 = 20.42$

   Using chart gives an APR of 18.5%.

8. Step 1: Find the amount financed.
   $7,588 - $2,588 = $5,000

   Step 2: Find the finance charge.
   $I = ($5,000)(.09)(3)$
   $I = $1,350$

   Step 3: Find the monthly payment.
   $\dfrac{$5,000 + $1,350}{36} = 176.39

   Step 4: Find the refund fraction.
   $S = \dfrac{36(37)}{2}$ \qquad $S = \dfrac{24(25)}{2}$

   $S = 666$ (denominator) $S = 300$ (numerator)
   Refund fraction = $\dfrac{300}{666}$

   Step 5: Calculate refund.
   $\dfrac{300}{666} \times $1,350 = 608.11 (refund)

   Step 6: Find total interest paid.
   $1,350 - $608.11 = $741.89

   Step 7: Find final payment. At time of 12th payment, 25 payments are due:

(25)($176.39)	$4,409.75
Less the refund	− $ 608.11
Equals	$3,801.64

   This represents the payoff.

9. Step 1: Find the refund fraction.

$$S = \frac{(15)(16)}{2} \qquad S = \frac{(9)(10)}{2}$$

$S = 120$ (denominator) $S = 45$ (numerator)

Refund fraction $= \dfrac{45}{120}$

Step 2: Find the refund.

$$\frac{45}{120} \times \$375 = \$140.63$$

Step 3: Find total interest paid.

$\$375 - \$140.63 = \$234.37$

Step 4: Find the final payment. At the time of the 6th payment, 10 payments are due:

(10)($225)	$2,250.00
Less refund	−$ 140.63
Equals	$2,109.37 (final payment)

10. a. $15,968 − $1,250 = $14,718

b. $I = (14{,}718)(.095)(3)$
$I = \$4{,}194.63$

c. $14,718 + $4,194.63 = $18,912.63

d. $\dfrac{\$18{,}912.63}{36} = \$525.35$

e. $\dfrac{\$4{,}194.63}{\$14{,}718} \times 100 = 28.5$

Using the chart or formula gives an APR of 17.00%.

f. Step 1: Calculate the refund fraction.

$$S = \frac{(36)(37)}{2} \qquad S = \frac{(21)(22)}{2}$$

$S = 666 \qquad\qquad S = 231$

Refund fraction $= \dfrac{231}{666}$

Step 2: Calculate the refund.

$$\frac{231}{666} \times \$4{,}194.63 = \$1{,}454.89$$

Step 3: Calculate the total interest paid.

$\$4,194.63 - \$1,454.89 = \$ 2,739.74$

Step 4: Find the final payment. At the time of the 15th payment, 22 payments are due:

(22)($525.35)	$11,557.70
Less refund	−$ 1,454.89
Equals	$10,102.81 (final payment)

ANSWERS TO PROBLEM SET 2

1. How to find after-tax cash flows each year:

Scheduled rental income (10)(8,500)	$85,000
Less vacancy and bad debts (.07)(85,000)	–$ 5,950
Plus miscellaneous income	+$ 0
Equals gross operating income	$79,050
Less operating expenses	–$22,000
Equals net operating income	$ 7,050
Less debt service	–$43,187
Equals before-tax cash flow	$13,863
Less taxes (or plus if tax savings)*	–$ 2,043
Equals after-tax cash flow	**$11,820**

Taxes from operation for each year:

Gross operating income	$79,050
Less operating expenses	–$22,000
Equals net operating income	$57,050
Less interest on debt	–$35,696
Less depreciation	–$14,545
Equals ordinary taxable income	$ 6,809
Times investor's tax rate (30%)	× .30
Equals taxes (or tax savings)	**$ 2,043**

2. The net proceeds from sale of an investment:

Expected selling price	$500,000
Less selling expenses	–$ 30,000
Less mortgage balances	–$325,000
Equals proceeds before taxes	$145,000
Less taxes due on sale*	–$ 33,600
Equals net proceeds after taxes	**$111,400**

Taxes due on sale of an investment

Original basis (purchase price)	$400,000
Plus capital improvements	+$ 48,000
Plus selling expenses	+$ 30,000
Less accumulated depreciation	–$ 90,000
Less partial sales	–$ 0
Equals adjusted cost basis	**$388,000**
Sale price	$500,000
Less adjusted cost basis	–$388,000
Equals taxable gain on sale	$112,000
Times investor's tax rate	× .30
Equals taxes due on sale	**$ 33,600**

3. **a.** Gross income multiplier = $\dfrac{\text{Value}}{\text{Gross operating income}}$

   Gross income multiplier = $\dfrac{\$450,000}{\$79,050}$

   Gross income multiplier = **5.69**

   b. Capitalization rate = $\dfrac{\text{Net operating income}}{\text{Value}}$

   Capitalization rate = $\dfrac{\$57,050}{\$450,000} \times 100$

   Capitalization rate = **12.68%**

4. Value = $\dfrac{\text{Net operating income}}{\text{Capitalization rate}}$

   Value = $\dfrac{\$57,050}{10.5\%}$

   Value = **$543,333.33**

5. **a.** $6.5 \times 30,000 =$ **$195,000**

   b. I = ($140,000)(.08)(1)
   I = **$11,200**

   c. $3,250 + $2,000 + $2,000 + $3,000 = **$10,250**

   d. $30,000 − $10,250 = **$19,750**

   e. $30,000 (income)
   −$10,250 (expenses)
   $19,750
   −$15,000 (debt service)
   $ 4,750

   f. $19,750
   −$11,200 (interest)
   $ 8,550
   −$ 4,909 (depreciation) $\dfrac{\$135,000}{27.5} = \textbf{\$4,909}$
   $ 3,641

   g. (1.04)($165,000) = **$171,600**

6. **a.** $12,000/.08 = $150,000

   b. $12,000/.11 = $109,091

   c. $12,000/.20 = $60,000

7. **a.** $8,500/$100,000 = 8.5%

   b. $8,500/$64,000 = 13.3%

   c. $8,500/$88,000 = 9.7%

8. **a.** ($85,000)(.85) = $7,225

   b. ($85,000)(.10) = $8,500

   c. ($85,000)(.12) = $10,200

9. **a.** 1/40 = .025 = 2.5%
   2.5% + 3.7% + 6% = 12.2%

   b. $10,000/.122 = $ 81,967

ANSWERS TO PROBLEM SET 3

1. Enter 500,000, hit FV.
   Enter 5, hit n.
   Enter 15, hit i.
   Hit PV.
   The value should be $248,588.37.

2. Two procedures.
   ($75,000)(1.05) = $78,750
   ($78,750)(1.05) = $82,687.50
   ($82,687.50)(1.05) = $86,821.88
   Or:
   Enter 75,000, hit PV.
   Enter 3, hit n.
   Enter 5, hit i.
   Hit FV.
   The value should be $86,821.88.

3. Enter 631.93, hit CHS, hit PMT.
   Enter 25, hit blue g key, hit n.
   Enter 12, hit blue g key, hit i.
   Hit PV.
   The value should be $59,999.57.

4. a. Enter 60, hit yellow f key, hit n (amort).
      Hit RCL, hit PV.
      The value should be $57,391.47.

   b. Enter 60, hit yellow f key, hit n (amort).
      Hit RCL, hit PV.
      The value should be $52,653.42.

5. Enter 1,340,000, hit FV.
   Enter 1,000,000, hit CHS, hit PV.
   Enter 6, hit n.
   Hit i.
   The value should be 4.9426, or about 5% per year.

6. a. Enter 1,000,000, hit PV.
      Enter 12.5, hit blue g key, hit i.
      Enter 20, hit blue g key, hit n.
      Hit PMT.
      The value should be $11,361.41.

   b. Enter 1,000,000, hit PV.
      Enter 12.5, hit i.
      Enter 20, hit n.
      Hit PMT.
      The value should be $138,095.73.

c.

Payment	Interest	Principal	Balance
1	$125,000.00	$13,095.73	$986,904.27
2	$123,363.03	$14,732.70	$972,171.57
3	$121,521.45	$16,574.28	$955,579.29
4	$119,449.66	$18,646.07	$936,951.22
5	$117,118.90	$20,976.83	$915,974.39

d. Enter 8, hit yellow f key, hit n(amort).
Hit RCL, hit PV.
The value should be $835,959.26.

7. Enter 450,000, hit PV.
Enter 5,417, hit CHS, hit PMT.
Enter 25, hit blue g key, hit n.
Hit i.
The value should be 1.17 (represents monthly rate).
Hit ENTER, enter 12, hit times keys.
The value should be 14.00%.

8.

Mortgage Payment

a. Enter 100,000, hit PV.
Enter 11, hit blue g key, hit i.
Enter 30, hit blue g key, hit n.
Hit PMT.
The payment is $952.32.

b. Enter 100,000, hit PV.
Enter 11, hit blue g key, hit i.
Enter 20, hit blue g key, hit n.
Hit PMT.
The payment is $1,032.19.

c. Enter 100,000, hit PV.
Enter 11, hit blue g key, hit i.
Enter 15, hit blue g key, hit n.
Hit PMT.
The payment is $1,136.60.

Total Interest

a. Enter 952.32, enter.
Enter 360, hit ✕.
342,835.20.
Enter 100,000, hit −.
242,835.20 (int.).

b. Enter 1,032.19, enter.
Enter 240, hit ✕.
247,725.60.
Enter 100,000, hit −.
110,566.76 (int.).

c. Enter 1,136.60, enter.
Enter 180, hit ✕.
204,588.00.
Enter 100,000, hit −.
104,588.00 (int.).

9.

Monthly Payment

a. Enter 100,000, hit PV.
Enter 8.5, hit blue g key, hit i.
Enter 20, hit blue g key, hit n.
Hit PMT.
The payment is $867.82.

b. Enter 100,000, hit PV.
Enter 9.5, hit blue g key, hit i.
Enter 20, hit blue g key, hit n.
Hit PMT.
The payment is $932.13.

Total Interest

a. Enter 867.82, enter.
Enter 240, hit ✕.
208,276.80.
Enter 100,000, hit −.
108,276.80 (int.).

b. Enter 932.13, enter.
Enter 240, hit ✕.
223,711.20.
Enter 100,000, hit −.
123,711.20 (int.).

c. Enter 100,000, hit PV.
Enter 11.5, hit blue g key, hit i.
Enter 20, hit blue g key, hit n.
Hit PMT.
The payment is $1,066.43.

c. Enter 1,066.43, enter.
Enter 240, hit ×.
255,943.20.
Enter 100,000,hit −.
155,943.20 (int.).

10. a. Enter 100,000, hit PV.
Enter 11.5, hit blue g key, hit i.
Enter 30, hit blue g key, hit n.
Hit PMT.
The payment is $990.29.
$990.29 × 360 = $356,504.40 Interest = $256,504.40
Enter 100,000, hit PV.
Enter 11.5, hit blue g key, hit i.
Enter 1040.29, hit CHS, hit PMT.
Hit n.
The term for payback is 267 months, or 22.25 years.
$1040.29 × 267 = $277,757.43 Interest = $177,757.43
Interest saved: $256,504.40 − $177,757.43 = $78,746.97

b. Enter 100,000, hit PV.
Enter 11.5, hit blue g key, hit i.
Enter 1090.29, hit CHS, hit PMT.
Hit n.
The term for payback is 222 months, or 18.5 years.
$1090.29 × 222 = $242,044.38 Interest = $142,044.38
Interest saved: $256,504.40 − $142,044.38 = $114,460.02

c. Enter 100,000, hit PV.
Enter 11.5, hit blue g key, hit i.
Enter 1,190.29, hit CHS, hit PMT.
Hit n.
The term for payback is 172 months, or 14.33 years.
1190.29 × 172 = 204,729.88 Interest = $104,729.88
Interest saved: $256,504.40 − $104,729.88 = $151,774.52

11. a. $8,616.77
Enter 5,000, CHS, hit PV.
Enter 11.5, hit i.
Enter 5, hit n.
Hit FV.
Use the same procedure for answers b and c, but substitute 10 and 25 for 5 in the third step.

b. $14,849.73

c. $76,004.92

12. a. $7,444.24
   Enter 100, hit CHS, hit PMT.
   Enter 8.5, hit blue g, hit i.
   Enter 5, hit blue g, hit n.
   Hit FV.
   Use the same procedure for answers b and c, but substitute 10 and 25 for 5 in the third step.

   b. $18,813.84

   c. $103,205.83

13. a. $852.28
   Enter 5,000, hit FV.
   Enter 8, hit i.
   Enter 5, hit n.
   Hit PMT.
   For answer b, substitute 10 for 8 in the second step.

   b. $818.99

14. a. $149,153.02
   Enter 300,000, hit FV.
   Enter 5, hit n.
   Enter 15, hit i.
   Hit PV.
   For answers b and c, substitute 10 and 25 for 5 in the second step.

   b. $74,155.41

   c. $ 9,113.29

15. a. $186,276.40
   Enter 300,000, hit FV.
   Enter 5, hit n.
   Enter 10, hit i.
   Hit PV.
   For answers b and c, substitute 10 and 25 for 5 in the second step.

   b. $115,662.99

   c. $ 27,688.80

16. a. $58,908.88
   Enter 6,000, hit CHS, hit PMT.
   Enter 20, hit n.
   Enter 8, hit i.
   Hit PV.
   For answers b and c, substitute 10 and 20 for 8 in the third step.

   b. $51,081.38

   c. $29,217.48

17. a. $76,072.74
  Enter 80,000, hit FV.
  Enter 20, hit n.
  Enter 8, hit i.
  Hit PV.
  The value should be $17,163.86.
  Enter 6,000, hit CHS, hit PMT.
  Enter 20, hit n.
  Enter 8, hit i.
  Hit PV, and the value should be 58,908.88.
  Add $17,163.86 and $58,908.88
  For answers b and c, substitute 10 and 20 for 8 in the third step.

  b. $11,891.49 + 51,081.38 = $62,972.87

  c. $2,086.72 + $29,217.48 = $31,304.20

18. a. $1,079.48
  Enter 80,000, hit PV.
  Enter 10.5, hit blue g key, hit i.
  Enter 10, hit blue g key, hit n.
  Hit PMT.
  For answers b and c, substitute 20 and 30 for 10 in the third step.

  b. $798.70

  c. $731.79

19. a. $50,222.61
  Enter 80,000, hit PV.
  Enter 10.5, hit blue g key, hit i.
  Enter 10, hit blue g key, hit n.
  Hit PMT.
  Enter 60, hit yellow f key, hit n (amort).
  Hit RCL, hit PV.
  For answers b and c, substitute 20 and 30 for 10 in the third step.

  b. $72,255.13

  c. $77,505.49

20. $1,915.00
  Enter 5,500, hit PV.
  Enter 10, hit blue g key, hit i.
  Enter 3, hit blue g key, hit n.
  Hit FV.
  The value should be $7,415.50.
  To find the interest, subtract the amount borrowed.

21. $1,820.00
  Enter 5,500, hit PV.
  Enter 10, hit i.
  Enter 3, hit n.
  Hit FV.
  The value should be $7,320.00.
  To find the interest, subtract the amount borrowed.

22. $3,558,180.62
    Enter 2,000, hit CHS, hit PMT.
    Enter 15, hit i.
    Enter 40, hit n.
    Hit FV.

23. $1,316.40
    Enter 20,000, hit FV.
    Enter 10, hit n.
    Enter 9, hit i.
    Hit PMT.

24. $74.85
    Enter 5,500, hit FV.
    Enter 5, hit blue g key, hit n.
    Enter 8, hit blue g key, hit i.
    Hit PMT.

25. $23,069.80
    Enter 51,000, hit FV.
    Enter 7, hit n.
    Enter 12, hit i.
    Hit PV.

26. $30,377.64
    Enter $1,000,000, hit FV.
    Enter 25, hit n.
    Enter 15, hit i.
    Hit PV.

27. $17,970.09
    Enter 3,000, hit CHS, hit FV.
    Enter 1, hit n.
    Enter 10.5, hit i.
    Hit PV.

28. $13,318.75
    Enter 3,000, hit FV.
    Enter 4, hit n.
    Enter 10, hit i.
    Hit PV.

29. $930.44
    Enter 7,500, hit PV.
    Enter 15, hit n.
    Enter 9, hit i.
    Hit PMT.

30. a. $46,047.56

Enter 50,000, hit PV.
Enter 10.25, hit i.
Enter 20, hit n.
Hit PMT.
Enter 4, hit yellow f key, hit n (amort).
Hit RCL, hit PV.

b. $31,580.31

Substitute 12 for 4 in fifth step.

31.

Year	Cash Flow	Discounted at 15%
0	($100,000)	($100,000.00)
1	$ 15,000	$ 13,043.48
2	$ 20,000	$ 15,122.87
3	$ 18,000	$ 11,835.29
4	$ 12,000	$ 6,861.04
5	$ 85,000	$ 42,260.02
Net present value:		**($ 10,877.30)**

32. Enter 100,000, hit CHS, hit blue g key, hit PV(CFo).
Enter 15,000, hit blue g key, hit PMT(CFj).
Enter 20,000, hit blue g key, hit PMT(CFj).
Enter 18,000, hit blue g key, hit PMT(CFj).
Enter 12,000, hit blue g key, hit PMT(CFj).
Enter 85,000, hit blue g key, hit PMT(CFj).
Hit yellow f key, hit FV(IRR).
The value should be 11.38%.

33. a. $77.73

Year 1:   Enter 25, hit FV.
Enter 1, hit n.
Enter 10, hit i.
Hit PV.
The value should be $22.73.

Year 2:   Enter 32, hit FV.
Enter 2, hit n.
Hit PV.
The value should be $26.45.

Year 3:   Enter 28, hit FV.
Enter 3, hit n.
Hit PV.
The value should be $21.04.

Year. 4:   Enter 11, hit FV.
Enter 4, hit n.
Hit PV.
The value should be $7.51.

The sum of the discounted values is $77.73.

b. $54.76

34. a. $10,000

 b. $0

 c. $45,000

 d. $40,000
 $100,000 – $50,000 = $50,000
 $50,000 – $5,000 = $45,000
 $45,000 – $5,000 = $40,000

 e. $24,836.84
 Enter 40,000, hit FV.
 Enter 10, hit i.
 Enter 5, hit n.
 Hit PV.

 f. 31.95%
 Enter 10,000, hit CHS, hit PV.
 Enter 40,000, hit FV.
 Enter 5, hit n.
 Hit i.

ANSWERS TO PROBLEM SET 4

These start on the next page.

1a.   ANNUAL PROPERTY OPERATING DATA

Name: <u>Mr. Jack the Investor</u>   Date: <u>   </u>
Property Address: <u>1234 Somewhere Dr.</u>   Price: <u>$164,000.00</u>
Type of Property: <u>6 unit apartment</u>   Equity: <u>$ 24,000.00</u>
                                                     Loans: <u>$140,000.00</u>

Assessed/Appraised Values

			Mortgage:	1st	2nd
Land:	$14,760.00	9.00%	Balance:	$ 90,000.00	$50,000.00
Improvement:	$149,240.00	91.00%	Int. Rate:	12.00%	10.50%
Personal Prop.:	$0.00	0.00%	Term:	20	20
Total:	$164,000.00	100.00%	Payment:	$990.98	$499.19

		1	2	3	Comments
1	SCHEDULED RENTAL INCOME			$25,200	Apt #1 $350
2	Less: Vacancy and Credit Losses			$1,260	Apt #2 $350
3	EFFECTIVE RENTAL INCOME			$23,940	Apt #3 $350
4	Plus: Other Income				Apt #4 $350
5	GROSS OPERATING INCOME			$23,940	Apt #5 $300
	less				Apt #6 $300
6	OPERATING EXPENSES				
7	Accounting		$0		
8	Advertising		$50		
9	Property Insurance		$400		
10	Property Management		$0		
11	Personal Property Taxes		$0		
12	School Taxes		$1,250		
13	Municipal & County Taxes		$350		
14	Repairs and Maintenance		$200		
15	Laundry		$0		
16	Lawn Care		$0		
17	Snow Removal		$100		
18	Legal		$0		
19	Licenses/Permits		$30		
20	Cable TV		$0		
21	Trash		$225		
22	Supplies		$0		
23	Electricity		$200		
24	Gas		$0		
25	Oil		$2,000		
26	Water and sewer		$600		
27	Telephone		$0		
28	Miscellaneous		$0		
29					
30	TOTAL OPERATING EXPENSES			$5,405	
	equals				
31	NET OPERATING INCOME			$18,535	
	less				
32	ANNUAL DEBT SERVICE			$17,882	
	equals				
33	BEFORE-TAX CASH FLOW			$653	

1a (cont.).

CASH FLOW ANALYSIS

Name: _____   Date: _____

MORTGAGE DATA

	Encumbrances	Beginning Balance	Remaining Term	Interest Rate	Monthly Payment	Annual Debt
1	1st Mortgage	$90,000	20	12.00%	$990.98	$11,891.73
2	2nd Mortgage	$50,000	20	10.50%	$499.19	$5,990.28

		Year 1	Year 2	Year 3	Year 4	Year 5
3	1st Mortgage Bal. (EOY)	$88,846	$87,546	$86,081	$84,430	$82,570
4	2nd Mortgage Bal. (EOY)	$49,223	$48,360	$47,403	$46,340	$45,159
5	Remaining Balance (EOY)	$138,069	$135,906	$133,484	$130,770	$127,729
6	Principal Paid (EOY)	$1,931	$2,163	$2,423	$2,714	$3,041
7	Total Interest (EOY)	$15,951	$15,719	$15,459	$15,168	$14,841

TAXABLE INCOME

		Year 1	Year 2	Year 3	Year 4	Year 5
8	Gross Operating Income	$23,940	$24,778	$25,645	$26,543	$27,472
	less					
9	Total Operating Expense	$5,405	$5,594	$5,790	$5,993	$6,202
	equals					
10	Net Operating Income	$18,535	$19,184	$19,855	$20,550	$21,270
	less					
11	Total Interest	$15,951	$15,719	$15,459	$15,168	$14,841
	less					
12	Depreciation	$5,427	$5,427	$5,427	$5,427	$5,427
	equals					
13	TAXABLE INCOME	($2,843)	($1,962)	($1,031)	($45)	$1,002

CASH FLOW AFTER TAXES

		Year 1	Year 2	Year 3	Year 4	Year 5
14	Net Operating Income	$18,535	$19,184	$19,855	$20,550	$21,269
	less					
15	Annual Debt Service	$17,882	$17,882	$17,882	$17,882	$17,882
	less					
16	Capital Additions	$0	$0	$0	$0	$0
	equals					
17	Cash Flow before Taxes	$653	$1,302	$1,973	$2,668	$3,387
	less					
18	Tax Liability	($1,095)	($756)	($397)	($17)	$385
	equals					
19	CASH FLOW AFTER TAXES	$1,748	$2,058	$2,370	$2,685	$3,002

1b. NET SALES PROCEEDS

Calculating Adjusted Cost Basis

1.	Original basis	$164,000
2.	Plus capital improvements	$0
3.	Plus selling expenses	$15,582
4.	Minus depreciation	$27,135
5.	Minus partial sales	$0
	Equals	
6.	Adjusted cost basis	**$152,447**

Calculating the Gain upon Sale

7.	Sales price	$194,781
8.	Minus adjusted cost basis	$152,447
	Equals	
9.	Capital gain	**$42,334**

Calculating the Tax on the Gain

10.	Capital gain	$42,334
11.	Times tax bracket	38.50%
	Equals	
12.	Total tax	$16,299

Calculating the Net Sales Proceeds

13.	Sales price	$194,781
14.	Minus selling expenses	$15,582
15.	Minus mortgage balances	$127,729
16.	Minus tax on gain	$16,299
	Equals	
17.	Net sales proceeds	$35,171

2a.   ANNUAL PROPERTY OPERATING DATA

Name: Apt. A

Property Address: _____

Type of Property: _____

Date:		
Price:	$ 50,000.00	
Equity:	$ 10,000.00	
Loans:	$ 40,000.00	

Assessed/Appraised Values

Land:	$0.00	0.00%
Improvement:	$0.00	0.00%
Personal Prop.:	$0.00	0.00%
Total:	$0.00	100.00%

Mortgage:	1st	2nd
Balance:	$40,000.00	$ 0
Int. Rate:	9.00%	10.50%
Term:	20	20
Payment:	$40,000.00	$0

		1	2	3	Comments
1	SCHEDULED RENTAL INCOME			$7,000	
2	Less: Vacancy and Credit Losses			$0	
3	EFFECTIVE RENTAL INCOME			$7,000	
4	Plus: Other Income				
5	GROSS OPERATING INCOME			$7,000	
	less				
6	OPERATING EXPENSES				
7	Accounting		$0		
8	Advertising		$0		
9	Property Insurance		$0		
10	Property Management		$0		
11	Personal Property Taxes		$0		
12	School Taxes		$0		
13	Municipal & County Taxes		$0		
14	Repairs and Maintenance		$0		
15	Laundry		$0		
16	Lawn Care		$0		
17	Snow Removal		$0		
18	Legal		$0		
19	Licenses/Permits		$0		
20	Cable TV		$0		
21	Trash		$0		
22	Supplies		$0		
23	Electricity		$0		
24	Gas		$0		
25	Oil		$0		
26	Water and sewer		$0		
27	Telephone		$0		
28	Miscellaneous		$2,000		
29					
30	TOTAL OPERATING EXPENSES			$2,000	
	equals				
31	NET OPERATING INCOME			$5,000	
	less				
32	ANNUAL DEBT SERVICE			$4,000	
	equals				
33	BEFORE-TAX CASH FLOW			$1,000	

2a (cont.).

<h1 style="text-align:center">CASH FLOW ANALYSIS</h1>

Name: <u>Apt. A</u>   Date: _____

MORTGAGE DATA

Encumbrances	Beginning Balance	Remaining Term	Interest Rate	Monthly Payment	Annual Debt
1	1st Mortgage	$40,000	not needed	9.00%	$0.00	$4,000.00
2	2nd Mortgage	$0	20	0.00%	$0.00	$0.00

		Year 1	Year 2	Year 3	Year 4	Year 5
3	1st Mortgage Bal. (EOY)	$39,600	$39,164	$38,689	$0	$0
4	2nd Mortgage Bal. (EOY)	$0	$0	$0	$0	$0
5	Remaining Balance (EOY)	$39,600	$39,164	$38,689	$0	$0
6	Principal Paid (EOY)	$400	$436	$475	$0	$0
7	Total Interest (EOY)	$3,600	$3,564	$3,525	$0	$0

TAXABLE INCOME

8	Gross Operating Income	$7,000	$7,350	$7,718	$0	$0
	less					
9	Total Operating Expense	$2,000	$2,100	$2,205	$0	$0
	equals					
10	Net Operating Income	$5,000	$5,250	$5,513	$0	$0
	less					
11	Total Interest	$3,600	$3,564	$3,525	$0	$0
	less					
12	Depreciation	$1,455	$1,455	$1,455	$0	$0
	equals					
13	TAXABLE INCOME	($55)	$231	$533	$0	$0

CASH FLOW AFTER TAXES

14	Net Operating Income	$5,000	$5,250	$5,513	$0	$0
	less					
15	Annual Debt Service	$4,000	$4,000	$4,000	$0	$0
	less					
16	Capital Additions	$0	$0	$0	$0	$0
	equals					
17	Cash Flow before Taxes	$1,000	$1,250	$1,513	$0	$0
	less					
18	Tax Liability	($17)	$69	$160	$0	$0
	equals					
19	CASH FLOW AFTER TAXES	$1,017	$1,181	$1,353	$0	$0

2a (cont.).

ANNUAL PROPERTY OPERATING DATA

Name: Apt. B

Property Address: _____

Type of Property: _____

Date: _____

Price: $ 80,000.00

Equity: $ 20,000.00

Loans: $ 60,000.00

Assessed/Appraised Values

Land:	$0.00	0.00%
Improvement:	$0.00	0.00%
Personal Prop.:	$0.00	0.00%
Total:	$0.00	100.00%

Mortgage:	1st	2nd
Balance:	$60,000.00	$0.00
Int. Rate:	9.00%	10.50%
Term:	20	20
Payment:	$ 9,000.00	$0.00

	1	2	3	Comments
1	SCHEDULED RENTAL INCOME		$11,000	
2	Less: Vacancy and Credit Losses		$0	
3	EFFECTIVE RENTAL INCOME		$11,000	
4	Plus: Other Income			
5	GROSS OPERATING INCOME		$11,000	
	less			
6	OPERATING EXPENSES			
7	Accounting	$0		
8	Advertising	$0		
9	Property Insurance	$0		
10	Property Management	$0		
11	Personal Property Taxes	$0		
12	School Taxes	$0		
13	Municipal & County Taxes	$0		
14	Repairs and Maintenance	$0		
15	Laundry	$0		
16	Lawn Care	$0		
17	Snow Removal	$0		
18	Legal	$0		
19	Licenses/Permits	$0		
20	Cable TV	$0		
21	Trash	$0		
22	Supplies	$0		
23	Electricity	$0		
24	Gas	$0		
25	Oil	$0		
26	Water and sewer	$0		
27	Telephone	$0		
28	Miscellaneous	$3,000		
29				
30	TOTAL OPERATING EXPENSES		$3,000	
	equals			
31	NET OPERATING INCOME		$8,000	
	less			
32	ANNUAL DEBT SERVICE		$9,000	
	equals			
33	BEFORE-TAX CASH FLOW		($1,000)	

2a (cont.).

CASH FLOW ANALYSIS

Name: <u>Apt. B</u>   Date: _____

MORTGAGE DATA

	Encumbrances	Beginning Balance	Remaining Term	Interest Rate	Monthly Payment	Annual Debt
1	1st Mortgage	$60,000	not needed	9.00%	$0.00	$9,000.00
2	2nd Mortgage	$0	20	0.00%	$0.00	$0.00

		Year 1	Year 2	Year 3	Year 4	Year 5
3	1st Mortgage Bal. (EOY)	$56,400	$52,476	$48,199	$0	$0
4	2nd Mortgage Bal. (EOY)	$0	$0	$0	$0	$0
5	Remaining Balance (EOY)	$56,400	$52,476	$48,199	$0	$0
6	Principal Paid (EOY)	$3,600	$3,924	$4,277	$0	$0
7	Total Interest (EOY)	$5,400	$5,076	$4,723	$0	$0

TAXABLE INCOME

		Year 1	Year 2	Year 3		
8	Gross Operating Income	$11,000	$11,660	$12,360	$0	$0
	less					
9	Total Operating Expense	$3,000	$3,180	$3,371	$0	$0
	equals					
10	Net Operating Income	$8,000	$8,480	$8,989	$0	$0
	less					
11	Total Interest	$5,400	$5,076	$4,723	$0	$0
	less					
12	Depreciation	$2,545	$2,545	$2,545	$0	$0
	equals					
13	TAXABLE INCOME	$55	$859	$1,721	$0	$0

CASH FLOW AFTER TAXES

14	Net Operating Income	$8,000	$8,480	$8,989	$0	$0
	less					
15	Annual Debt Service	$9,000	$9,000	$9,000	$0	$0
	less					
16	Capital Additions	$0	$0	$0	$0	$0
	equals					
17	Cash Flow before Taxes	($1,000)	($520)	($11)	$0	$0
	less					
18	Tax Liability	$17	$258	$516	$0	$0
	equals					
19	CASH FLOW AFTER TAXES	($1,017)	($778)	($527)	$0	$0

3a.   ANNUAL PROPERTY OPERATING DATA

Name: 4-Unit
Property Address: _____
Type of Property: _____

Date: 1990
Price: $140,000.00
Equity: $ 20,000.00
Loans: $120,000.00

Assessed/Appraised Values

Land:	$0.00	0.00%
Improvement:	$0.00	0.00%
Personal Prop.:	$0.00	0.00%
Total:	$0.00	100.00%

Mortgage:	1st	2nd
Balance:	$120,000.00	$0.00
Int. Rate:	11.50%	10.50%
Term:	20	20
Payment:	$15,565.00	$0.00

	1	2	3	Comments
1	SCHEDULED RENTAL INCOME		$21,000	
2	Less: Vacancy and Credit Losses		$1,050	
3	EFFECTIVE RENTAL INCOME		$19,950	
4	Plus: Other Income			
5	GROSS OPERATING INCOME		$19,950	
	less			
6	OPERATING EXPENSES			
7	Accounting	$0		
8	Advertising	$0		
9	Property Insurance	$0		
10	Property Management	$0		
11	Personal Property Taxes	$0		
12	School Taxes	$0		
13	Municipal & County Taxes	$0		
14	Repairs and Maintenance	$0		
15	Laundry	$0		
16	Lawn Care	$0		
17	Snow Removal	$0		
18	Legal	$0		
19	Licenses/Permits	$0		
20	Cable TV	$0		
21	Trash	$0		
22	Supplies	$0		
23	Electricity	$0		
24	Gas	$0		
25	Oil	$0		
26	Water and sewer	$0		
27	Telephone	$0		
28	Miscellaneous	$6,500		
29				
30	TOTAL OPERATING EXPENSES		$6,500	
	equals			
31	NET OPERATING INCOME		$13,450	
	less			
32	ANNUAL DEBT SERVICE		$15,565	
	equals			
33	BEFORE-TAX CASH FLOW		($2,115)	

3a (cont.).

CASH FLOW ANALYSIS

Name: <u>4-Unit</u>   Date: _____

MORTGAGE DATA

	Encumbrances	Beginning Balance	Remaining Term	Interest Rate	Monthly Payment	Annual Debt
1	1st Mortgage	$120,000	20	11.50%	$0.00	$15,565.00
2	2nd Mortgage	$0	20	0.00%	$0.00	$0.00

		Year 1	Year 2	Year 3	Year 4	Year 5
3	1st Mortgage Bal. (EOY)	$118,235	$116,267	$114,073	$0	$0
4	2nd Mortgage Bal. (EOY)	$0	$0	$0	$0	$0
5	Remaining Balance (EOY)	$118,235	$116,267	$114,073	$0	$0
6	Principal Paid (EOY)	$1,765	$1,968	$2,194	$0	$0
7	Total Interest (EOY)	$13,800	$13,597	$13,371	$0	$0

TAXABLE INCOME

		Year 1	Year 2	Year 3	Year 4	Year 5
8	Gross Operating Income	$19,950	$20,948	$21,995	$0	$0
	less					
9	Total Operating Expense	$6,500	$6,825	$7,166	$0	$0
	equals					
10	Net Operating Income	$13,450	$14,123	$14,829	$0	$0
	less					
11	Total Interest	$13,800	$13,597	$13,371	$0	$0
	less					
12	Depreciation	$5,055	$5,055	$5,055	$0	$0
	equals					
13	TAXABLE INCOME	($5,405)	($4,529)	($3,597)	$0	$0

CASH FLOW AFTER TAXES

		Year 1	Year 2	Year 3	Year 4	Year 5
14	Net Operating Income	$13,450	$14,123	$14,829	$0	$0
	less					
15	Annual Debt Service	$15,565	$15,565	$15,565	$0	$0
	less					
16	Capital Additions	$0	$0	$0	$0	$0
	equals					
17	Cash Flow before Taxes	($2,115)	($1,442)	($736)	$0	$0
	less					
18	Tax Liability	($1,513)	($1,268)	($1,007)	$0	$0
	equals					
19	CASH FLOW AFTER TAXES	($602)	($174)	$271	$0	$0

3a (cont.). ANNUAL PROPERTY OPERATING DATA

Name: 6-Unit

Property Address: _____

Type of Property: _____

Date:	1990		
Price:	$152,000.00		
Equity:	$ 25,000.00		
Loans:	$127,000.00		

Assessed/Appraised Values

Land:	$0.00	0.00%
Improvement:	$0.00	0.00%
Personal Prop.:	$0.00	0.00%
Total:	$0.00	100.00%

Mortgage:	1st	2nd
Balance:	$127,000.00	$0.00
Int. Rate:	11.00%	10.50%
Term:	20	20
Payment:	$15,948.00	$0.00

		1	2	3	Comments
1	SCHEDULED RENTAL INCOME			$25,100	
2	Less: Vacancy and Credit Losses			$1,757	
3	EFFECTIVE RENTAL INCOME			$23,343	
4	Plus: Other Income				
5	GROSS OPERATING INCOME			$23,343	
	less				
6	OPERATING EXPENSES				
7	Accounting		$0		
8	Advertising		$0		
9	Property Insurance		$0		
10	Property Management		$0		
11	Personal Property Taxes		$0		
12	School Taxes		$0		
13	Municipal & County Taxes		$0		
14	Repairs and Maintenance		$0		
15	Laundry		$0		
16	Lawn Care		$0		
17	Snow Removal		$0		
18	Legal		$0		
19	Licenses/Permits		$0		
20	Cable TV		$0		
21	Trash		$0		
22	Supplies		$0		
23	Electricity		$0		
24	Gas		$0		
25	Oil		$0		
26	Water and sewer		$0		
27	Telephone		$0		
28	Miscellaneous		$6,800		
29					
30	TOTAL OPERATING EXPENSES			$6,800	
	equals				
31	NET OPERATING INCOME			$16,543	
	less				
32	ANNUAL DEBT SERVICE			$15,948	
	equals				
33	BEFORE-TAX CASH FLOW			$595	

3a (cont.).

CASH FLOW ANALYSIS

Name: <u>6-Unit</u>   Date: _____

MORTGAGE DATA

	Encumbrances	Beginning Balance	Remaining Term	Interest Rate	Monthly Payment	Annual Debt
1	1st Mortgage	$127,000	20	11.00%	$0.00	$15,948.00
2	2nd Mortgage	$0	20	0.00%	$0.00	$0.00

		Year 1	Year 2	Year 3	Year 4	Year 5
3	1st Mortgage Bal. (EOY)	$125,022	$122,826	$120,389	$0	$0
4	2nd Mortgage Bal. (EOY)	$0	$0	$0	$0	$0
5	Remaining Balance (EOY)	$125,022	$122,826	$120,389	$0	$0
6	Principal Paid (EOY)	$1,978	$2,196	$2,437	$0	$0
7	Total Interest (EOY)	$13,970	$13,752	$13,511	$0	$0

TAXABLE INCOME

		Year 1	Year 2	Year 3	Year 4	Year 5
8	Gross Operating Income	$23,343	$24,160	$25,006	$0	$0
	less					
9	Total Operating Expense	$6,800	$7,038	$7,284	$0	$0
	equals					
10	Net Operating Income	$16,543	$17,122	$17,722	$0	$0
	less					
11	Total Interest	$13,970	$13,752	$13,511	$0	$0
	less					
12	Depreciation	$6,041	$6,041	$6,041	$0	$0
	equals					
13	TAXABLE INCOME	($3,468)	($2,671)	($1,830)	$0	$0

CASH FLOW AFTER TAXES

		Year 1	Year 2	Year 3	Year 4	Year 5
14	Net Operating Income	$16,543	$17,122	$17,721	$0	$0
	less					
15	Annual Debt Service	$15,948	$15,948	$15,948	$0	$0
	less					
16	Capital Additions	$0	$0	$0	$0	$0
	equals					
17	Cash Flow before Taxes	$595	$1,174	$1,773	$0	$0
	less					
18	Tax Liability	($971)	($748)	($513)	$0	$0
	equals					
19	CASH FLOW AFTER TAXES	$1,566	$1,922	$2,286	$0	$0

3a (cont.). ANNUAL PROPERTY OPERATING DATA

Name: 8-Unit

Property Address: _____

Type of Property: _____

Date: 1990

Price: $160,000.00

Equity: $ 25,000.00

Loans: $135,000.00

Assessed/Appraised Values

Land:	$0.00	0.00%
Improvement:	$0.00	0.00%
Personal Prop.:	$0.00	0.00%
Total:	$0.00	100.00%

Mortgage:	1st	2nd
Balance:	$135,000.00	$0.00
Int. Rate:	9.50%	10.50%
Term:	25	20
Payment:	$15,200.00	$0.00

	1	2	3	Comments
1	SCHEDULED RENTAL INCOME		$24,100	
2	Less: Vacancy and Credit Losses		$1,205	
3	EFFECTIVE RENTAL INCOME		$22,895	
4	Plus: Other Income			
5	GROSS OPERATING INCOME		$22,895	
	less			
6	OPERATING EXPENSES			
7	Accounting	$0		
8	Advertising	$0		
9	Property Insurance	$0		
10	Property Management	$0		
11	Personal Property Taxes	$0		
12	School Taxes	$0		
13	Municipal & County Taxes	$0		
14	Repairs and Maintenance	$0		
15	Laundry	$0		
16	Lawn Care	$0		
17	Snow Removal	$0		
18	Legal	$0		
19	Licenses/Permits	$0		
20	Cable TV	$0		
21	Trash	$0		
22	Supplies	$0		
23	Electricity	$0		
24	Gas	$0		
25	Oil	$0		
26	Water and sewer	$0		
27	Telephone	$0		
28	Miscellaneous	$6,895		
29				
30	TOTAL OPERATING EXPENSES		$6,895	
	equals			
31	NET OPERATING INCOME		$16,000	
	less			
32	ANNUAL DEBT SERVICE		$15,200	
	equals			
33	BEFORE-TAX CASH FLOW		$800	

3a (cont.).

CASH FLOW ANALYSIS

Name: **8-Unit** _____   Date: _____

MORTGAGE DATA

	Encumbrances	Beginning Balance	Remaining Term	Interest Rate	Monthly Payment	Annual Debt
1	1st Mortgage	$135,000	25	9.50%	$0.00	$15,200.00
2	2nd Mortgage	$0	20	0.00%	$0.00	$0.00

		Year 1	Year 2	Year 3	Year 4	Year 5
3	1st Mortgage Bal. (EOY)	$132,625	$130,024	$127,177	$0	$0
4	2nd Mortgage Bal. (E0Y)	$0	$0	$0	$0	$0
5	Remaining Balance (EOY)	$132,625	$130,024	$127,177	$0	$0
6	Principal Paid (EOY)	$2,375	$2,601	$2,848	$0	$0
7	Total Interest (EOY)	$12,825	$12,599	$12,352	$0	$0

TAXABLE INCOME

8	Gross Operating Income	$22,895	$23,925	$25,002	$0	$0
	less					
9	Total Operating Expense	$6,895	$7,205	$7,530	$0	$0
	equals					
10	Net Operating Income	$16,000	$16,720	$17,472	$0	$0
	less					
11	Total Interest	$12,825	$12,599	$12,352	$0	$0
	less					
12	Depreciation	$6,493	$6,493	$6,493	$0	$0
	equals					
13	TAXABLE INCOME	($3,318)	($2,372)	($1,373)	$0	$0

CASH FLOW AFTER TAXES

14	Net Operating Income	$16,000	$16,720	$17,472	$0	$0
	less					
15	Annual Debt Service	$15,200	$15,200	$15,200	$0	$0
	less					
16	Capital Additions	$0	$0	$0	$0	$0
	equals					
17	Cash Flow before Taxes	$800	$1,520	$2,272	$0	$0
	less					
18	Tax Liability	($929)	($664)	($384)	$0	$0
	equals					
19	CASH FLOW AFTER TAXES	$1,729	$2,184	$2,656	$0	$0

ANSWERS TO PROBLEM SET 5

1.	Year	ATCF	Net Proceeds	10% Discount	20% Discount
	0	($80,000)			
	1	$10,000		$ 9,091	$ 8,333
	2	$20,000		$16,529	$13,889
	3	$20,000		$15,026	$11,574
	4	$25,000	$50,000	$51,226	$36,169
				$91,872	$69,965

a. NPV at 10% = ($80,000) + $91,872 = +11,872
   The discount rate is too low.

b. NPV at 20% = ($80,000) + $69,965 = –10,035
   The discount rate is too high.
   The internal rate of return is between 10% and 15%.

c. 14.93%
   Enter 80,000, hit CHS, hit blue g key, hit PV(CFo).
   Enter 10,000, hit blue g key, hit PMT(CFj).
   Enter 20,000, hit blue g key, hit PMT(CFj).
   Enter 20,000, hit blue g key, hit PMT(CFj).
   Enter 75,000, hit blue g key, hit PMT(CFj).
   Hit yellow f key, hit FV(IRR).

d. To prove this is the correct IRR, discount cash flows at 14.93%:

10,000	$ 8,701
20,000	$15,141
20,000	$13,174
75,000	$42,984
	$80,000

2. $102,127.08. Two methods on calculator.

Year	Cash Flow	Discount at 15%
1	$ 10,000	$ 8,695.65
2	$ 10,500	$ 7,939.51
3	$ 12,000	$ 7,890.19
4	$ 11,000	$ 6,289.29
5	$ 13,000	$ 6,463.30
6	$150,000	$ 64,849.14
		$102,127.08

Enter 0, hit blue g key, hit PV(CFo)
Enter 10,000, hit blue g key, hit PMT(CFj).
Enter 10,500, hit blue g key, hit PMT(CFj).
Enter 12,000, hit blue g key, hit PMT(CFj).
Enter 11,000, hit blue g key, hit PMT(CFj).
Enter 13,000, hit blue g key, hit PMT(CFj).
Enter 150,000, hit blue g key, hit PMT(CFj).
Hit yellow f key, hit PV(NPV).

3. 18.06%
   Use the information from the cash flow sheets.

Year	Cash Flow
0	($100,000)
1	$ 14,433
2	$ 15,567
3	$ 16,727
4	$ 17,911
5	$ 19,120 plus $112,150

Enter 100,000, hit CHS, hit blue g key, hit PV(CFo).
Enter 14,433, hit blue g key, hit PMT(CFj).
Enter 15,567, hit blue g key, hit PMT(CFj).
Enter 16,727, hit blue g key, hit PMT(CFj).
Enter 17,911, hit blue g key, hit PMT(CFj).
Enter 131,270, hit blue g key, hit PMT(CFj).
Hit yellow f key, hit FV(IRR).

3. (*cont.*)   ANNUAL PROPERTY OPERATING DATA

Name: Chapter 5—Problem 3

Property Address: 1234 Somewhere Dr.

Type of Property: 28-unit apartment

Date:	1994	
Price:	$500,000.00	
Equity:	$100,000.00	
Loans:	$400,000.00	

Assessed/Appraised Values

Land:	$75,000.00	15.00%
Improvement:	$425,000.00	85.00%
Personal Prop.:	$0.00	0.00%
Total:	$500,000.00	100.00%

Mortgage:	1st	2nd
Balance:	$400,000.00	$0.00
Int. Rate:	10.00%	10.50%
Term:	25	20
Payment:	$44,067.23	$0.00

		1	2	3	Comments
1	SCHEDULED RENTAL INCOME			$115,920	
2	Less: Vacancy and Credit Losses			$8,114	
3	EFFECTIVE RENTAL INCOME			$107,806	
4	Plus: Other Income				
5	GROSS OPERATING INCOME			$107,806	
	less				
6	OPERATING EXPENSES				
7	Accounting		$0		
8	Advertising		$0		
9	Property Insurance		$0		
10	Property Management		$0		
11	Personal Property Taxes		$0		
12	School Taxes		$0		
13	Municipal & County Taxes		$0		
14	Repairs and Maintenance		$0		
15	Laundry		$0		
16	Lawn Care		$0		
17	Snow Removal		$0		
18	Legal		$0		
19	Licenses/Permits		$0		
20	Cable TV		$0		
21	Trash		$0		
22	Supplies		$0		
23	Electricity		$0		
24	Gas		$0		
25	Oil		$0		
26	Water and sewer		$0		
27	Telephone		$0		
28	Miscellaneous		$48,000		
29					
30	TOTAL OPERATING EXPENSES			$48,000	
	equals				
31	NET OPERATING INCOME			$59,806	
	less				
32	ANNUAL DEBT SERVICE			$44,067	
	equals				
33	BEFORE-TAX CASH FLOW			$15,739	

3. (*cont.*)

CASH FLOW ANALYSIS

Name: <u>Chapter 5—Problem 3</u>   Date: _____

MORTGAGE DATA

	Encumbrances	Beginning Balance	Remaining Term	Interest Rate	Monthly Payment	Annual Debt
1	1st Mortgage	$400,000	25	10.00%	$0.00	$44,067.23
2	2nd Mortgage	$0	20	10.50%	$0.00	$0.00

		Year 1	Year 2	Year 3	Year 4	Year 5
3	1st Mortgage Bal. (EOY)	$395,933	$391,459	$386,537	$381,124	$375,169
4	2nd Mortgage Bal. (EOY)	$0	$0	$0	$0	$0
5	Remaining Balance (EOY)	$395,933	$391,459	$386,537	$381,124	$375,169
6	Principal Paid (EOY)	$4,067	$4,474	$4,921	$5,413	$5,955
7	Total Interest (EOY)	$40,000	$39,593	$39,146	$38,654	$38,112

TAXABLE INCOME

		Year 1	Year 2	Year 3	Year 4	Year 5
8	Gross Operating Income less	$107,806	$111,040	$114,371	$117,802	$121,336
9	Total Operating Expense equals	$48,000	$49,440	$50,923	$52,451	$54,025
10	Net Operating Income less	$59,806	$61,600	$63,448	$65,351	$67,311
11	Total Interest less	$40,000	$39,593	$39,146	$38,654	$38,112
12	Depreciation equals	$15,454	$15,454	$15,454	$15,454	$15,454
13	TAXABLE INCOME	$4,352	$6,553	$8,848	$11,243	$13,745

CASH FLOW AFTER TAXES

		Year 1	Year 2	Year 3	Year 4	Year 5
14	Net Operating Income less	$59,806	$61,600	$63,448	$65,351	$67,311
15	Annual Debt Service less	$44,067	$44,067	$44,067	$44,067	$44,067
16	Capital Additions equals	$0	$0	$0	$0	$0
17	Cash Flow before Taxes less	$15,739	$17,533	$19,381	$21,284	$23,244
18	Tax Liability equals	$1,306	$1,966	$2,654	$3,373	$4,124
19	CASH FLOW AFTER TAXES	$14,433	$15,567	$16,727	$17,911	$19,120

3. (*cont.*)

NET SALES PROCEEDS

Calculating Adjusted Cost Basis

1.	Original basis	$500,000
2.	Plus capital improvements	$0
3.	Plus selling expenses	$35,000
4.	Minus depreciation	$77,270
5.	Minus partial sales	$0
	Equals	
6.	Adjusted cost basis	$457,730

Calculating the Gain upon Sale

7.	Sales price	$550,000
8.	Minus adjusted cost basis	$457,730
	Equals	
9.	Capital Gain	$92,270

Calculating the Tax on the Gain

10.	Capital gain	$92,270
11.	Times tax bracket	30.00%
	Equals	
12.	Total tax	$27,681

Calculating the Net Sales Proceeds

13.	Sales price	$550,000
14.	Minus selling expenses	$35,000
15.	Minus mortgage balances	$375,169
16.	Minus tax on gain	$27,681
	Equals	
17.	Net sales proceeds	$112,150

4. a. $10,000

    b. $7,300 (rental income)
        <u>–$1,000</u> (taxes)
        $6,300
        <u>–$6,300</u> (interest only: 9% of $70,000)
        $ 0

    c. $120,000
        <u>–$ 8,400</u> (selling costs)
        $111,600
        <u>–$ 70,000</u> (mortgage balance)
        $ 41,600

    d. $41,600
        <u>–$ 8,000</u> (taxes)
        $33,600

    e. $20,862.96
        Enter 33,600, hit FV.
        Enter 10, hit i.
        Enter 5, hit n.
        Hit PV.

    f. 27.43%
        Enter 33,600, hit FV.
        Enter 10,000, hit CHS, hit PV.
        Enter 5, hit n.
        Hit i.

5. a. $22,697.07
        Enter 40,000, hit FV.
        Enter 12, hit i.
        Enter 5, hit n.
        Hit PV.

    b. $16,075.10
        Enter 40,000, hit FV.
        Enter 20, hit i.
        Enter 5, hit n.
        Hit PV.

    c. 14.87%
        Enter 20,000, hit CHS, hit PV.
        Enter 40,000, hit FV.
        Enter 5, hit n.
        Hit i.

6. a. $25,824.42
        Enter 240,000, hit PV.
        Enter 20, hit n.
        Enter 8.75, hit i.
        Hit PMT.

    b. $211,270.72

   c. $100,392.82

Enter 5, hit yellow f key, hit n (amort).
The value should be 100,392.82.
Hit RCL, hit PV.
The value should be 211,270.72.

7. a. $20,000

   b.

Gross income	$15,000
Operating expenses	–$ 5,640
	$ 9,360
Debt service	–$ 9,500
Before-tax cash flow	($140)

   c. $91,885.81

Enter 95,000, hit PV.
Enter 9,500, hit CHS, hit PMT.
Enter 9, hit i.
Hit n.
The value should be 27.
Enter 3, hit yellow f key, hit n(amort).
Hit RCL, hit PV.

   d. $ 30,646.19

$140,000.00
–$ 9,800.00 (selling expenses)
$130,200.00
–$ 91,885.81 (mortgage balance)
$ 38,314.19
–$ 7,668.00 (tax on the sale)
$ 30,646.19

8. a. 14.73%

Enter 20,000, hit CHS, hit blue g key, hit PV(CFo).
Enter 6,000, hit CHS, hit blue g key, hit PMT(CFj).
Enter 6,000, hit CHS, hit blue g key, hit PMT(CFj).
Enter 6,000, hit CHS, hit blue g key, hit PMT(CFj).
Enter 6,000, hit CHS, hit blue g key, hit PMT(CFj).
Enter 74,000, hit blue g key, hit PMT(CFj).
Hit yellow f key, hit FV(IRR).

   b. 12.72%

Year	Cash Flow	
0	($20,000)	$20,000.00
1	($ 6,000) discounted at 8%	$ 5,555.55
2	($ 6,000) discounted at 8%	$ 5,144.03
3	($ 6,000) discounted at 8%	$ 4,762.99
4	($ 6,000) discounted at 8%	$ 4,410.18
5	($ 6,000) discounted at 8%	$ 4,083.50
Amount needed for investment is		$43,956.25

c. 16.74%

Intitial investment $20,000
$6,000 borrowed at 10% for 4 years = $ 8,785
$6,000 borrowed at 10% for 3 years = $ 7,986
$6,000 borrowed at 10% for 2 years = $ 7,260
$6,000 borrowed at 10% for 1 years = $ 6,600
$6,000 borrowed at 10% for 0 years = $ 6,000
Total amount due $56,631
Net proceeds = $80,000 – $56,631 = $23,369
Enter 20,000, hit CHS, hit PV.
Enter 23,369, hit FV.
Enter 5, hit n.
Hit i.

9. a. See the Cash Flow Analysis on page 127.

b. 15.74%

($4,890) discounted at 8% = ($4,528)
($4,895) discounted at 8% = ($4,197)
($4,900) discounted at 8% = ($3,890)
($4,906) discounted at 8% = ($3,606)
Initial investment necessary $20,000 + $16,221
Initial investment necessary $36,221
Enter 36,221, hit CHS, hit PV.
Enter 65,000, hit FV.
Enter 4, hit n.
Hit i.

c. 20.09%

($4,890) borrowed at 12% for 3 years = ($ 6,870)
($4,895) borrowed at 12% for 2 years = ($ 6,140)
($4,900) borrowed at 12% for 1 year = ($ 5,488)
($4,906) borrowed at 12% for 0 years = ($ 4,906)
Total amount due at time of sale   ($23,404)
Therefore:
Net proceeds = $ 65,000 – $23,404 = $41,596
Enter 20,000, hit CHS, hit PV.
Enter 41,596, hit FV.
Enter 4, hit n.
Hit i.

CASH FLOW ANALYSIS

Name: <u>Chapter 5—Problem 9</u>   Date: _____

MORTGAGE DATA

	Encumbrances	Beginning Balance	Remaining Term	Interest Rate	Monthly Payment	Annual Debt
1	1st Mortgage	$65,000	25	8.00%	$0.00	$5,400.00
2	2nd Mortgage	$0	20	10.50%	$0.00	$0.00

		Year 1	Year 2	Year 3	Year 4	Year 5
3	1st Mortgage Bal. (EOY)	$64,800	$64,584	$64,351	$64,099	$63,827
4	2nd Mortgage Bal. (EOY)	$0	$0	$0	$0	$0
5	Remaining Balance (EOY)	$64,800	$64,584	$64,351	$64,099	$63,827
6	Principal Paid (EOY)	$200	$216	$233	$252	$272
7	Total Interest (EOY)	$5,200	$5,184	$5,167	$5,148	$5,128

TAXABLE INCOME

8	Gross Operating Income	$0	$0	$0	$0	$0
	less					
9	Total Operating Expense	$1,500	$1,500	$1,500	$1,500	$1,500
	equals					
10	Net Operating Income	($1,500)	($1,500)	($1,500)	($1,500)	($1,500)
	less					
11	Total Interest	$5,200	$5,184	$5,167	$5,148	$5,128
	less					
12	Depreciation	$0	$0	$0	$0	$0
	equals					
13	TAXABLE INCOME	($6,700)	($6,684)	($6,667)	($6,648)	($6,628)

CASH FLOW AFTER TAXES

14	Net Operating Income	($1,500)	($1,500)	($1,500)	($1,500)	($1,500)
	less					
15	Annual Debt Service	$5,400	$5,400	$5,400	$5,400	$5,400
	less					
16	Capital Additions	$0	$0	$0	$0	$0
	equals					
17	Cash Flow before Taxes	($6,900)	($6,900)	($6,900)	($6,900)	($6,900)
	less					
18	Tax Liability	($2,010)	($2,005)	($2,000)	($1,994)	($1,988)
	equals					
19	CASH FLOW AFTER TAXES	($4,890)	($4,895)	($4,900)	($4,906)	($4,912)

10. a. 14.13%

$3,800 in year 1 earns interest at 5.5% for 2 years ($4,229.50).
$4,200 in year 1 earns interest at 5.5% for 1 year ($4,431.00).
Total in account at end of two years is $8,660.50.
Subtract negative flow of $2,200; then $6,460.50 will earn interest at 5.5% for one year.
Total in account at end of 3 years is $6,815.83.
Subtract negative flow of $3,600; then $3,215.83 will earn interest at 5.5% for one year.
Total in the account at the end of 4 years is $3,392.70.
This is not enough to cover the negative flow of $5,600; so the investor must cover ($2,207.30).
Discounting $2,207.30 at 5.5% for 5 years yields $1,688.88, which is additional money needed to be set aside as part of the initial investment.

Enter 21,688.88, hit CHS, hit PV.
Enter 42,000, hit FV.
Enter 5, hit n.
Hit i.

b. 14.56%

$3,800 at 5.5% for 4 years	$4,707.53
$4,000 at 8% for 3 years	$4,931.81
($2,200) at 9.5% for 2 years	($2,637.86)
($3,600) at 9.5% for 1 year	($3,942.00)
($5,600) at 9.5% for 0 years	($5,600.00)

Net proceeds = $42,000 + $4,707.53 + $4,931.81 – $2,637.86 – $3,942.00 – $5,600

Net proceeds = $ 39,459.48
Enter 20,000, hit CHS, hit PV.
Enter 39,459.48, hit FV.
Enter 5, hit n.
Hit i.

INDEX